Herbs and spices have always been a [...] life. The younger son of John and Rosemary Hemphill, who pioneered Australia's love of herbs and spices in the 1950s, Ian would earn his pocket money picking herbs on the family farm, Somerset Cottage. He remembers many a season when their home was strewn with bunches of drying culinary produce. Ian worked with his parents for many years, managed a spice company in Singapore and was a senior manager for a multinational food company in Australia. In 1997 Ian and his wife Elizabeth opened a specialty spice shop in the Sydney suburb of Rozelle, which bears the nickname Ian has had since school days – Herbie's. In 2000 Herbie's Spices was the winner of the Australian Gourmet Traveller Jaguar Award for Excellence for Innovation in Produce.

Ian and Elizabeth continue to enjoy sharing their passion for spices through the shop, spice appreciation classes and taking groups to India on an annual Spice Discovery Tour.

Also by Ian Hemphill

Spice Notes: A cook's compendium of herbs and spices

SPICE

A spice merchant's voyage of discovery

TRAVELS

IAN HEMPHILL

MACMILLAN
Pan Macmillan Australia

First published in 2002 in Macmillan by Pan Macmillan Australia Pty Limited
St Martins Tower, 31 Market Street, Sydney

National Library of Australia
cataloguing-in-publication data:

Hemphill, Ian R. (Ian Rupert), 1949– .
Spice travels: a spice merchant's voyage of discovery.

ISBN 0 7329 1151 6.

1. Hemphill, Ian R. (Ian Rupert), 1949– . – Journeys. 2. Condiments.
3. Voyages and travels. 4. Spice trade. 5. Trade routes. I. Title

910.4

Typeset in 13 pt Griffo Classico by Post Pre-press Group
Printed in Australia by McPherson's Printing Group
Cover and text design: Deborah Parry Graphics
Cover photograph: Ian Hemphill

Extract from *The Moor's Last Sigh* by Salman Rushdie published by Jonathan Cape.
Used by permission of The Random House Group Limited.

For my parents, John and Rosemary Hemphill

Contents

BROTHERHOOD of SPICE MERCHANTS

In 1986, I discovered I was not alone.

To explain this awakening I should start with a brief history of my experiences with herbs and spices up until that time. My parents started one of the first herb nurseries in Australia in the late 1950s, so I had been associated with the business of herbs and spices my whole life. As a child, herbs were all around me. In those days in Australia, herbs were something of an oddity, and more than a few people who drove the 50 kilometres from Sydney to the rural landscape of Dural expected to see my mother dressed in witch's garb, stooped over a steaming cauldron of spellbinding herbs. The reality was quite different. My parents' property, Somerset Cottage, was set within manicured lawns, with a stonewalled herb garden and a quaint fairytale cottage with a high-pitched roof. Here they sold an array of herbs and herb-related merchandise. I grew up in this fragrant, colourful and flavoursome environment. Herbs and business were the familiar topics for dinner-table conversation and I would earn pocket money by helping Dad propagate cuttings, serving customers or picking and stripping herbs ready for drying.

Thousands of customers made the trip to Dural each year to see our herb garden. And one of the questions they most often asked us was, 'What is the difference between a herb and a spice?' Although some professional opinions may differ slightly, it is generally accepted that, in culinary terms, a herb is the leafy part of a plant. Any other parts of plants are called spices. Spices can be the buds (cloves), bark (cinnamon), roots (ginger), berries (peppercorns), aromatic seeds (cumin), and even the stigma of a flower in the case of saffron. Many of the aromatic seeds we call spices are actually gathered from 'herb' plants when they have finished flowering. A familiar example is coriander, the leaves being referred to as a herb, whereas the dried seeds are always called a spice. So one may ask, 'What about the stem and roots of coriander that are used in cooking, and of onions, garlic and the delicious bulb of fennel?' These sections of vegetable matter tend to be classified along with herbs. Therefore when a cook is adding ingredients such as coriander leaves, lemongrass stalk, garlic and coriander roots they would all be referred to as the *herbs*. The cumin, pepper, chilli, galangal, turmeric and ginger may be referred to as the *spices*.

Our company became the first in this country to sell a complete range of bottled culinary herbs and spices in supermarkets. Our range was comprised of forty-eight varieties in those days, about double that of anyone else. However, we were no match for the multinational herb and spice companies.

Their presence in Australia and practice of 'buying' shelf-space decimated our supermarket business. We then began exporting, quite successfully, to Singapore and Malaysia. Our Singapore distributor was taken over by a company that had recently acquired a spice business in Singapore, and looking for a managing director, they approached us with a view to buying our business. It was not an easy decision, but Dural had lost its attraction as a tourist destination and was developing into an outer suburb of Sydney. Also, dozens of shops around the country had picked up Mum's creative, and until then unique, way of presenting herbs and spices, books, preserves, fragrant items, garden ornaments, herbal teas and so much more. So in a life-changing moment, Liz and our three girls came with me to Singapore, and Mum and Dad prepared for retirement.

I had been working in the herbs and spices industry for sixteen years in 1986, and yet it was only over the preceding two years that I had really begun to discover the depth and diversity that permeates this ancient trade. At that stage I thought I knew quite a lot about culinary herbs and spices. Although I had been involved in growing, processing and packing most herbs, I had only read about the same aspects relating to spices. While I had blended and packed tonnes of pepper, turmeric, chilli, cardamom, cinnamon and nutmeg over the years, I had never seen any of these growing or being processed. The company I managed sold a range of retail packs in supermarkets and ground spices to food manufacturers in Singapore, Malaysia and the Philippines. We employed a food technologist and over many weeks I learnt more than I ever thought there was to know about the different grades and methods of processing spices.

To understand some of these dynamics better I wanted

to see how businesses, other than the one I was managing, processed their spices. With this aim in mind I visited a small spice-grinding business in Jurong, Singapore, that was owned by an Indian family. They specialised in grinding chillies imported from India, Pakistan and China, and exported many tonnes of ground chillies. The atmosphere in the concrete, lichen-stained factory was a cross between a Dickensian work-house and a seventeenth-century godown. The workers were stripped to their waists, wearing only the *longyi* (a sarong with the back hem pulled up between the legs and tucked into the waist at the front, to create what looks like baggy trousers). Five 'Heath Robinson' spice grinders churned away noisily, reducing sacks of bright red chillies to a red-orange powder.

Because the mechanical action of grinding generates so much heat, the chilli powder has to be cooled when it comes out of the grinder, otherwise it can scorch and discolour. To prevent this, great piles of eye-watering chilli powder were spread out to cool on the concrete floor. After the powder was raked up by the sweating, barefooted workers standing ankle deep in it, it was returned to the grinders for a second grinding to make it extra fine. Another stage of raking out and cooling took place before final bagging.

After about twenty minutes my ears were ringing from the constant clattering of the grinders, and although my nose and eyes were streaming, I was mesmerised by the sweet, fruity aroma and lingering, burning sensation of chilli. I was starting to understand that even though our hygienic, state-of-the-art facility in Pandan Loop was superior to this somewhat primi-tive operation, it was essential to my education to see a process in its most basic form. Then I was able to fully appreciate it.

This was the first of many excursions to fuel my curiosity about spices. No matter how much I knew, I would always discover some interesting tidbit that made me want to find out even more. In Singapore my investigations had to be conducted at lunchtime so I could indulge in a banana leaf curry at the notorious Muthu's curry house. It was not long after this that Muthu's was involved in a scandal that hit the headlines in *The Straits Times*. Someone had been murdered and the body was hidden in a vat of curry sauce at Muthu's. Although the owners were exonerated in the case, patrons who remembered the headlines depicting the 'Muthu's Curry Murder' never returned. Fortunately there were plenty of other banana leaf restaurants in Serangoon Road, so I was able to support my developing habit.

The banana leaf curry is named after the banana leaf it is served on. At a good restaurant, a *doti*-wearing waiter will place the banana leaf in front of you and shovel a few tablespoons of rice onto it. They will then bring to your table four or five wire-handled tiffin tins (the size of small paint tins) and dish out from each one a spoonful or two of tasty morsels around your pile of rice. Rich lamb curry, cabbage with brown mustard seeds, potatoes and cumin, tandoori marinated prawns, dry beef curry and sambar, all complemented by a glass of *rasam* (pepper water) to pour over the rice. From a selection of smaller tins there are accompaniments such as lime pickles, green and red chilli, green mango, turmeric and tamarind. I still cannot for the life of me eat a meal like this slowly. Whether eaten with a spoon and fork or in the traditional way with one's fingers, the heavenly taste sensation of a spiced meal such as this convinces me that God really must be an Indian.

Seven months after moving to Singapore, and to my astonishment, the Singapore Manufacturers' Association nominated me, an expatriate Australian, to be their representative at the first meeting of the International Spice Group in New Delhi.

India is the acknowledged home of spices, and although I would be barely scratching the surface, this trip felt like a pilgrimage. During the flight there and over subsequent years, the web-like fascination that India holds for many a traveller began to weave its enchantment around my psyche.

Safely through customs at around midnight, and eventually negotiating my way through the baggage collection process, I was out of the airport and looking for a cab to take me into New Delhi. I have travelled in many parts of Asia on business and experienced the tuk-tuks of Thailand, the beaten-up old Corollas of Jakarta, the stretch Mercedes in Hong Kong, and the immaculately clean Toyota Crown taxis of Singapore. But I had never really experienced a taxi ride until I had made my first journey in India's Ambassador motorcar. The Ambassador is a 1950s Morris Oxford, made in India and based on dies bought from the British when they stopped manufacturing them. Although mechanically some changes have been made, the body style of Ambassador cars made today is exactly the same as it was in the fifties.

Completing the taxi experience is the driver. I knew which hotel I had to go to and in the early hours of a cool November morning with the streets uncharacteristically abandoned, I set off from the airport. My wild-eyed driver sported a scarf around his head tied at the nape of his neck like a ponytail, giving him a distinctly piratical appearance. His unorthodox driving position did nothing to bolster my confidence. Travelling in an Ambassador at 60 kilometres per hour feels like 120, and I could only assume that his oblique lean was in readiness for the next corner, when we would be consigned to two wheels. Taking the bends, he perched bolt upright while I floundered on the shiny red vinyl and cream-piped upholstery in the back.

To my surprise I arrived safely at the Ashoka Hotel – a marble edifice in a very grand style and although quite new, the carpets, timberwork and furnishings had a decidedly frayed countenance. I was welcomed by Mr Thampi, an officer from the Spices Board of India, who was looking after publicity for the conference. The delegate's notes he gave me announced the auspicious event at which I was to present my paper in the following terms:

> Personate to the International Symposium on the Export Development of Spices (London, 24–26 October 1979) and the Consultative Meeting on Spices (Geneva, 24–26 May 1983), the First Meeting of the International Spice Group is held in New Delhi during 24–29 November 1986, jointly convened and organized by the Commonwealth Secretariat and The International Trade Center UNCTAD/GATT (ITC). The Government of India has provided host facilities for the meeting.

Something inside told me this event was to be a milestone. In the late 1950s and early sixties herbs and spices were 'new' and my parents' herb garden was something of a curiosity. Although the women's magazines and leading-light foodies of the day were enthralled by what my mother and father were doing, for a child it was somewhat peculiar and more often a source of ridicule from one's peers than the basis for admiration. So much so that in my latter years at school I earned the nickname 'Herbie' which, at the time I was not terribly impressed with, but it has stuck to me throughout my working life. So here I was at the age of thirty-seven amongst a brotherhood of spice merchants, agricultural ministers from Jamaica, the Seychelles, Madagascar and Tanzania, the British, Canadian and Nigerian High Commissioners, and agricultural researchers who special-ised in herbs and spices. It was akin to finding a tribe that one had been orphaned from at an early age and upon being reunited, discovering a common language.

This was the moment I knew I was not alone.

Presentations were made about production, processing and research and development for spices, however what made this trip truly memorable were the out-of-conference times. Coming down to breakfast on the first morning I was met by a tantalising, some-what smoky aroma filling the air. Was this the pollution of thousands of home cooking fires around Delhi or simply the hotel incinerator? No, it was the smell of the tandoor, and as I descended to the dark-panelled hotel restaurant my nostrils were bombarded with a symphony of food fragrances from the warm, doughy, slightly burnt naan bread to a distinctive roasted, cumin-scented potato with coriander overtones. These competed for olfactory attention with lentils slow-cooked with garam masala, curry leaves, and teased with asafoetida. The aroma of a rich curry sauce thickened with *channa dhal* flour wafted by, and at once I knew this was the land where my soul belonged.

I joined Fazli Husain from the International Trade Centre in Geneva, who was tucking into his vegetarian break-fast. Fazli was a man of strong convictions and often railed at the hypocrisy of nations that criticised developing countries for their poverty and lack of hygiene standards, while they ignored their own poverty-stricken vagrants and slum areas as if they simply did not exist.

The camaraderie and discussions with my fellow delegates made this trip most poignant. An Englishman by the name of Phil Button took me under his wing and in a matter of days he had made me aware of how little I knew of the trade. Phil was widely travelled, had been a buyer for a large British spice company and now, in semi-retirement, he was working as a consultant. Under his dour and somewhat gruff exterior was a desire to pass on his knowledge.

Phil told me about such things as the difference between Madras and Alleppey turmeric, and how the British prefer the Madras type because it is paler and has less flavour. Every now and then he would throw a tricky question at me to see if I had been listening. Did I know about spice extracts and how spent spices are sometimes used as an adulterant? I knew a little about extracts because many food manufacturers, especially those producing smallgoods, had begun using them instead of natural spices. The extracts would be free from bacteria and the flavour strength would be standardised, making it no longer necessary to adjust recipes to allow for seasonal flavour strength variations. I never liked this idea of using extracts, because much of the joy in using spices comes from their natural textures, which contribute to the eating experience.

On the last afternoon of the conference the organisers hired a couple of buses and took some of the overseas delegates on a sight-seeing trip of New Delhi and Old Delhi. Visiting the Red Fort, built by Shah Jahan in 1648, and the typically Indian hubbub of touts, hawkers, beggars and opportunists surrounding its entrance, was a mind-boggling experience. Old Delhi is an assault on the senses for a first-time visitor to India, but I loved its dynamism. New Delhi, where the conference was being held, is a comparatively ordered, planned city with wide, tree-lined streets. Nonetheless it is very Indian and for all its planning it still has an atmosphere as thick as molasses. A simple stroll along the streets here becomes an adventure filled with sounds, sights, aromas and experiences which was very exciting for this simple Aussie bloke. We walked around the concentric roads and radiating streets of Connaught Place in New Delhi, where we saw three young men painting a traffic light pole with rags dipped in bright yellow paint. I think there was more paint on their hands and clothes than on the pole. I found a stationery shop that was piled high with cloth-bound, hard-cover exercise books that would have looked more at home in the eighteenth century than in the twentieth.

As I flew back to Singapore, enchanted by my experience of one tiny part of India, I braced myself to drop back into the reality of corporate life. Within four years I would be free from these shackles and would, with my dear wife Liz, be taking a group of a dozen travellers to Sri Lanka and India on our first Spice Discovery Tour. In the years ahead we would become consumed by an insatiable appetite to seek out more and more spice experiences, all around the world. We developed a thirst for knowledge that would be momentarily quenched until the desire to discover the inside story on another spice emerged. Each journey has inflamed our passion for spices, and heightened our fascination with this ancient trade.

But WHERE is STANLEY'S FARM?

A common misconception about the spice trade is that spices are grown in accessible, orderly plantations that one can readily visit. The reality is, the majority of spices are produced by individual farmers, who grow and harvest relatively small quantities in areas that are remote and difficult to find. So when we planned our first Spice Discovery Tour in 1991, we had only a vague idea of what would really be involved in undertaking an exercise as seemingly straightforward as 'finding Stanley's farm to see cinnamon'.

It all began early in 1990 when Liz said to me, 'What we need,' on her hobbyhorse again, 'is to show people where the spices actually grow. It seems that people think pepper comes from a packet, not a vine. It's like kids who think milk comes from bottles because they've never seen a cow. Wouldn't it be wonderful to take people to see cinnamon being peeled, to make the world of spices really come alive?'

As it happened, we were speaking to Lesley Richardson, the Vice-President of the Food Media Club at the time. Her husband, whom we'd only just met, said calmly, 'That's easy. I'm a travel agent, and my speciality is group tours and I have a lot of experience with travel in India and Sri Lanka. I can put it together for you.'

We soon discovered that the notion of mounting a three-week tour structured to visit as many spice-producing areas as possible, and accommodating up to fifteen travellers, was a daunting task. Besides the arrangements that would have to be made to find suitable farms, brochures would have to be printed and the tour would need to be advertised and pro-moted. Fortunately, the Australian food division of Unilever, which marketed the Clive of India brand of curry powders, agreed to sponsor us. The tour was promoted by way of a brochure calling upon interested travellers to 'Enter the exciting and historic world of Clive of India, the British East India Company and the exotic spices that drew early explorers to India, in this fully guided twenty-one-day tour.' We promised to show the difference between black, green, white and pink peppercorns and to leave the beaten tourist tracks to find fragrant cinnamon and other spices. Because of Liz's love of elephants, the cover of our leaflet featured an ambling file of these noble creatures at the Amber Fort in Jaipur. By the time we departed Australia in the first week of March 1999 there were fourteen 'spice tourists' booked for our adventure.

We flew to Colombo via Singapore, a ten-hour journey that landed us in the Sri Lankan capital at three in the morning. Unknown by us at that time, the Sri Lankan Deputy Minister for Defence and Security had been assassinated the day that we had been travelling. A 50 kilogram bomb had killed about sixty people and injured many more. The story went that the Deputy Minister had been instrumental in foiling a criminal group engaged in foreign currency fraud, and they had vowed to get even . . . and did. It appeared that the authorities believed the perpetrator of this crime had Singapore connections, so all luggage being transported from Singapore had to undergo stringent examination – so thorough, in fact, that they didn't have time to get it all done before the plane took off! The result was that not one, or maybe two, but *eleven* of the suitcases belonging to our group did not arrive when we did. Imagine how we felt – tired, disoriented, and faced with apparent indifference to our plight.

Each one of us who had lost baggage had to have a 'baggage irregularity report' completed in triplicate. A beautiful young woman gazed impassively at our distress. She was completely unflappable, and filled in forms with careful and ponderous deliberation. The young man working beside her was not nearly so composed. He empathised with our misfortune, but no matter how much he desperately tried to help us, his attempts at speed and efficiency only served to create a flurry of papers. One excitable member of our group was ready to take the place apart, and was gearing up to have the full wrath of the heavens descend upon the small group of polite but ineffectual Sri Lankan airport officials who were still there at this ungodly hour of the morning. As time went on with no resolution, a well-connected member of our group was keen to contact the Singapore justice minister – a friend of his – to get him to jump on the airline company. Fortunately a representative of the airline made himself useful at last by handing out

first-class overnight bags containing soap and a toothbrush, tis-
sues and dressing gown. Small comfort, though, when we were
all looking forward to a shower and a change of clothes.

It was a disastrous beginning to our adventure. Why
had we taken on this ridiculous idea? Liz and I looked at our
group of charges, either dejected or angry, all tired, and wondered what else would go wrong in the next three weeks. After
about two hours, our guide, Walter, showed us to our bus,
assuring us that nothing further could be achieved so early in
the morning and that we would love Sri Lanka, which means
'resplendent island'. Walter was voluble, charming and always
interesting, and over the next two days we would become
totally reliant on him.

Everyone was in surprisingly good spirits after our short
sleep. The fact that the hotel was comfortable, the breakfast
delicious and the shops promising probably had a lot to do with
it, and the loss of luggage had begun to be seen in the light of a
good story back home. A traveller's tale, no matter how awful
at the time, makes for great conversation for years to come.

In our little bus, presided over by Walter, we headed
south, passing the famous but now jaded Galle Face Hotel.
Colombo was like no other city I had seen. There was a drastic
lack of traffic lights, kerbing, footpaths, municipal garbage bins
and department stores. We proceeded along the main arterial
road out of the city past open-fronted stores which appeared to
be little more than shacks, yet had a timeless permanence about
them. Progress was slow and it took us two hours to drive
through the commercial areas, each one with its own specialty
– basketware, furniture, silks and saris, plumbing items and
accessories – and lots of timberyards. Everywhere I looked

there was a scrawny dog or two – were all the dogs identical, I wondered, or was I seeing the same few fifty times?

Occasionally, we passed beautiful traditional houses, a sort of cement-rendered colonial. Sadly, most of them were fairly run-down, an appearance that we have come to expect in these tropical climates where fresh rendering and paint are quickly attacked by the ravages of black moulds and algae. One building that particularly took our attention was a barn made completely of thatch. At unexpected moments, we glimpsed clown-faced monkeys with sombre secrets in their eyes staring out at us from the jungle growing alongside the road.

We were fascinated to see large trucks, unevenly sprung and listing, with wooden cabins painted in the most amazing and complicated designs of colourful flowers and scenes depicting gods and goddesses hovering above Eden-like landscapes. Their incongruous bright blues and shades of orange were speckled with drifts of glitter. Many of them carried up to fifty passengers standing in the back and were heavily decorated with fresh flowers.

'They are pilgrims,' Walter told us. 'The flowers are betel nut flowers and palm fronds. They are tied to the front of a bus or a truck to signify pilgrimage.' I suppose they hoped that in the event of a road accident as they hurtled along in this apparently reckless fashion, their gods would recognise the vehicle most deserving of protection.

Our first spice encounter was at Silva's cinnamon processing yard, a considerable commercial enterprise about half the size of an Australian suburban block. The proprietor, a Mr Gamini Silva, who was initially bemused by this group of Australians who had travelled halfway around the world to see something as common as cinnamon, showed us several grades of cinnamon quills that are purchased from about ten different growers. Collectively they produce about 50 tonnes of cinnamon a season. The 'Hamburg' grades 1, 2 and 3 are the most readily available, with a stronger flavour, while the 'Mexican' grades 4 and 5 have a milder taste.

It might have been a stupid question, but we had to ask why it was called 'Mexican cinnamon' when it grows in Sri Lanka. The reason is that Mexico is the world's largest single customer for cinnamon, buying about two-thirds of the annual production of Sri Lanka. The grade preferred by Mexico is naturally enough named for them. Similarly, the 'Hamburg' grade is the standard most commonly exported to Europe.

Gamini showed us how the metre-long quills are graded according to quality of flavour and aroma, and on how well the quills have been rolled. Damaged cinnamon that is not visually appealing is referred to as 'foxed'. The quills are then either roped together in 50 kilogram bales in the same time-honoured manner as has been performed for centuries, or cut with what looks like a handyman's bench circular saw, into the universal-standard 8 centimetre lengths we all see when we buy cinnamon quills.

To the delight of everyone in the group, Gamini presented each of us with a bundle of 'Mexican' grade 5. Ranjit Silva, the manager, explained that the whole quills were cut to a standard length depending on the customer's requirements, and the 'quillings' or 'featherings' (broken and feathery pieces) were used along with the 'Hamburg' grade 3 and foxed cinnamon for grinding into powder.

'Where do you grind it?' I asked, anxious to get a close

look at some serious machinery and taking in the storage room piled full of bales of cinnamon. 'I don't see a grinder.' Ranjit explained that they hire a grinding machine when they need it, in the same way that Australian farmers may hire or share expensive pieces of machinery like combine harvesters. Interesting as this was to me, the attention of some members of our group was beginning to waver – my enthusiasm for the minutiae of spice detail is not always shared. To everyone's delight, we were distracted by a wizened, loincloth-clad gentleman and his elephant taking the morning shopping home in a blue plastic bag held in the elephant's trunk. Obligingly, he steered his placid animal into the driveway of the cinnamon yard so that we could all enjoy this moment of Sri Lankan daily routine.

This elephant was about forty-five years old, and had been with his current owner's family all its life. It is a sign of great wealth to own an elephant, which was worth then about 500,000 rupees or A\$16,000. When elephants are not working in the timber industry, their owners sometimes rent them out for temple engagements, and often when an elephant is seen walking along a country road, it is on its way to one of these temple jobs. It is more economical for the temples, as many of them simply can't afford to own their own animals.

After visiting the cinnamon processing plant, we were keen to find out how cinnamon was turned into those tightly rolled sticks. 'After lunch we're taking you to Stanley's farm to see cinnamon being peeled,' Walter assured us. Although I had read many accounts of cinnamon peeling, I was looking forward to actually seeing it done, but first lunch sounded like a good idea.

Our tummies were rumbling as the bus bumped along

the road to Ahungalla. Suddenly we turned into the gateway of the stunning Triton Hotel, leaving the stalls, garbage heaps and straggling pedestrians behind. We found ourselves on a long, immaculate driveway lined with palms and lawns, which skirted a huge pool dotted with islands upon which clusters of palm trees were growing. As the bus drew up in front of the hotel, we could see straight through the wide foyer to a vista of the beach and ocean which was upstaged by another pool that seemed to merge with the sea. I had been brought up with the Sunday-school wisdom of building your house upon the rock and not upon the sand, yet here they'd built not only a magnificent hotel but also these enormous pools right on the beach.

Eagerly we stepped from the bus and, skirting lobster-shaded German and Italian tourists lying on towels like abandoned inflatable pool toys, we headed for the bar. I took orders from the group and then relayed to the bar attendant, 'Eleven beers, please.' We collapsed with laughter when we were solemnly presented with eleven full-sized bottles of beer, all opened. We dealt with them easily in Sri Lanka's tropical humidity and followed them with a fabulous smorgasbord of local food.

This was an eclectic mix of spiced local dishes and stodgy potato, cauliflower, pasta and cheese to cater for the hotel's European guests. We loved the vegetable and dhal curries, and had our first encounter with dry fish curry. As the name suggests, the fish is quite dry and even crisp around the edges from what we would consider to be overcooking, but in no time we acquired a liking for this typically Sri Lankan and South Indian way of preparing seafood. I am pleased to say our group pounced on the local fare with gusto, all determined to make the most of this experience and not miss out on anything.

We were happy to see that the members of the group were getting to know each other and it appeared we'd been lucky. It's a gamble to throw people who've never met before together for three weeks, and as the time went by, we were to discover that we couldn't have had a more pleasant group of people if we'd handpicked each one of them.

After lunch we were keen to get to Stanley's farm to see the cinnamon peeling. The bus turned off the Galle Road on to a dirt road barely wide enough for it, and occasionally we'd stop so that the driver could lean out the window to ask directions of a local. In the machine-gun-fire rapidity of the Sinhalese language, we'd identify the word 'Stanley' and see an arm confidently waving us on, further down the road. Eventually the driver asked again at a small post office station, and someone offered to direct us, so we followed his car. We turned into a well-kept driveway, and once again the driver leaned out and asked some women weeding around trees, 'Stanley?', much nodding and pointing, 'Yes, Stanley, up the drive.'

We parked the bus beside a small farmhouse, and a puzzled-looking family straggled out and stared at us, speechless. Walter had a quick consultation with them. It appeared the farmer had never heard of Stanley, but good-naturedly agreed to demonstrate cinnamon peeling. His wife, the grandmother and two daughters fetched chairs from the house and arranged them on the verandah for us while the farmer and another man went and cut a few one-metre branches from the cinnamon trees (*Cinnamomum zeylanicum*). Normally the harvest begins in May, so these sticks were a little young.

The men sat on the concrete floor of the verandah, and with a small curved blade they scraped the soft outer bark from the just-cut cinnamon and discarded it, leaving the dusky, slightly lemon-scented layer beneath it intact. Using a small brass rod, they vigorously rubbed up and down the stick, bruising and loosening the remaining bark from the inner core of wood. With one end of the cinnamon stick gripped between big toe and second toe, and using a dangerous-looking, scalpel-sharp blade, one of the men cut a long line down the length of the stick and proceeded to gently prise the soft, tan bark away. As it magically lifted off in long tubes, he passed it to his companion, who became 'quill monitor', telescoping more perfect gutters together, creating the familiar joins one sees in cinnamon quills. He kept packing smaller pieces inside the original tube until it was stuffed with many concentric layers of extremely thin bark.

While we watched this act of skill with wonder, Walter told us how cinnamon grades are affected by climate, seasons and soil quality. He also said that this cinnamon peeler would take five hours to peel 3 kilograms of cinnamon, and in the peak season, this farm would employ somewhere between twenty and sixty workers. The long, round quills would be dried on racks for three or four days, then rolled again and put in the sun for a day or two. The drying setup for the cinnamon quills was a series of nails at ceiling height inside the cottage. Strings were tied from one nail to another on the opposite side of the room, forming a grid. The cinnamon was laid across the strings to make a fragrant ceiling. The wood that remains after the bark is removed is used for fuel and to make incense, but retains little useful aroma. The leaves from the cinnamon tree are used like bay leaves, and are often referred to in Indian and Sri Lankan recipes as 'Indian bay leaves' or 'tejpat'. These leaves have a distinctly clove-like aroma and taste. If you have a recipe that calls for them, it is better to use a whole clove as a substitute rather than a European bay leaf, which tastes completely different.

We begged a spare unpeeled stick of cinnamon from the hospitable farmer. He probably thought we were crazy, but the hotel gardener who was called upon later to cut it into suitcase-sized lengths thought so even more!

A storm broke as we returned to Colombo, and the traffic was reduced to a crawl. Walter took us to a batik factory where he obviously got a percentage from the sales, something we came to discover is normal practice, and those of us who had lost our luggage bought some clothes. We asked Walter to take us to a store where we could buy underwear – a fairly futile task late on a Sunday afternoon, but he eventually found a tiny general clothing shop. The lost baggage arrived and was delivered to the hotel in time for us to check out.

When we arrived at the airport, the good news was that people who had been forced to buy clothing would be re-imbursed. The bad news was that our bookings on to Madras had been deleted from the computer because they had not been re-confirmed. 'How did this happen?' I asked, trying to remain calm.

'You failed to reconfirm your bookings,' I was told.

We retraced the events of our arrival. Because the flight from Singapore had been delayed and it was three o'clock on Sunday morning when we arrived, and the airline office was closed on Sunday, it was impossible to confirm our following flight. As a result our bookings had been summarily cancelled.

Liz tends to describe me as a gentle soul, the very

essence of tolerance and reason – most of the time. Without losing my cool, without shouting or ranting, I became very, very angry, and it was not pleasant for the airline to be on the receiving end. The result was that our entire group of sixteen was miraculously reinstated onto the scheduled flight.

The SPICES
RESEARCH STATION

Where else in the world but India would you find a Spices
Research Station? Fortunately for those of us who are consumed by the lifelong passion for all things associated with
spices, India takes this subject very seriously. More so, in fact,
than any other country in the world. Therefore when we took
our Spice Discovery Tour to India in March 1991, it would not
have been complete without a visit to the Spices Research
Station in Ahmedabad in the north-western state of Gujarat.
Our objective was to see where agricultural research is undertaken for India's seed spices. While spices gathered from the
roots, fruits, berries, bark and buds of plants, shrubs and trees
tend to come from the tropical zones north and south of the
equator, seed spices are mostly grown in the temperate zones
further north and south. Although trade over many centuries
has made most spices obtainable even in remote areas, in

regional cuisines there is a tendency to favour those spices that are most readily available. So in the south of India, pepper, cardamom, ginger and turmeric will dominate, while in the north there is the frequent use of fenugreek, cumin, dill, ajowan, fennel, mustard and coriander seeds.

The flight to Ahmedabad had taken us via a short stopover in Mumbai, which is the post-colonial name for Bombay. The drive from the airport to the hotel in the city provided more culture shocks for our group of intrepid travellers. Our rattly old bus crawled through almost stationary traffic, while around us, the incredible crush of humanity was fascinating, exciting and disturbing. We passed families who lived permanently on the footpaths surrounded by their possessions or in humpies made of hessian bags. Cows with arched horns, pointed tips painted blue, wandered amongst the throng, seemingly oblivious to the honking horns, trucks, bicycles and pedestrians weaving around them. A rustic, hand-pulled cart carrying the body of an old man trundled by the bus window. Some of us could not avert our eyes from this unfamiliar sight. Others looked away out of respect for the departed. This is India, a contradiction of emotion, fascination, voyeurism, cynicism, beauty and pragmatism, all assaulting the senses at once. Arriving at the majestic Taj Mahal Hotel, which overlooks India Gate, we entered a cool, comfortable haven away from the heat and intensity of the city.

While appreciating this calm retreat, Liz and I felt ashamed at our cowardice by indulging in such comfort while there was so much out there to see. So we ventured forth early the next morning as the crowds stirred and the nearby markets were beginning to open. We strolled through these markets and wondered when the streets were ever used to convey traffic, as they were crammed with stalls selling a wonderful variety of good quality fresh fruits and vegetables. We couldn't help noticing how many vegetables looked smaller than our highly fertilised, irrigated produce back home. After tasting these humble offerings, though, I noticed they conveyed a richness of flavour that reminded me of Dad's home-grown vegetables. We passed a barrow as large as a small utility truck, piled high with potent, tiny, white garlic bulbs (*Allium sativum*). At another stall there were little tomatoes, not the trendy cherry tomatoes we know, but ones that would be shunned in our supermarkets for lack of size. However, each one seemed to have as much flavour in its compact sphere as two mass-produced tomatoes double the size.

Liz spotted a large brass bucket that we couldn't resist buying for about A\$15. We then proceeded to fill it with gee-gaws and bric-a-brac for our little girls. Next stop was the fish markets, which thankfully, at the cool beginning of the day, had not yet developed their characteristic pong. Fish of all sizes were on sale, neatly laid out by merchants who sat cross-legged behind their silvery displays of gutted offerings. A buyer haggled with the merchant, who with fish-scale-encrusted, calloused hands turned a shiny carcass to reveal its fresh appearance, while trying to convince his customer that it was good value. We hurried past the cleaning area, entrails slithering between deft, knife-wielding workers' feet as they fell on the concrete floor, before being shovelled away.

By now my head was starting to spin from all that was going on around us, so we took respite at a small 'hotel' – hotels in the streets here being more like cafés than hostelries. Weak black tea lightly spiced with cardamom refreshed us while we spread out our purchases for the girls.

As we flew to Ahmedabad in the north-west of India, we recalled our experiences in Hyderabad to the east, which we had visited on our journey between Colombo and Mumbai, and wondered how they would be different. By contrast, Hyderabad we believed to be relatively wealthy, something confirmed upon our arrival there. The Hyderabad Oberoi struck us as something between the Shangri-la of *Lost Horizon* and Nirvana. We were greeted by acres of marbled high ceilings, solid carved wooden doors, highly polished marble in the bathrooms, expansive open areas, a swimming pool and panoramic views. Our guide in Hyderabad, Satish, had not experienced a group that wanted to go bush rather than linger over local sights, such as the magnificent Golconda Fort. Satish had done his homework, though, and we headed out of town with a picnic lunch packed by the hotel. The bus lurched to a halt in front of a Muslim arms shop and as Satish alighted we joked about whether he was collecting an issue of weapons for our protection. Nothing so dramatic, he emerged with two enormous red rugs for us to sit on when we had our lunch.

Travelling further out of Hyderabad the traffic had thinned, horns blared less frequently and the crowds became less dense. Our first stop was at a jasmine garden where marigolds, roses and chrysanthemums were also growing. The jasmine was tied up like a bush, so the flowers would grow prolifically on the outside for easy picking. Flowers are an important part of Indian life. Whether they are used for devotional purposes, or worn by married Hindu women in their hair every day, or for sheer pleasure, blossoms are on sale daily in every market. The aroma of cut flowers was intoxicating as their fragrances spread into the warming morning air and evoked in me a deep childhood memory. It was in the mid 1960s when my father made potpourri from rose petals, various scented-leaved geraniums, lavender and calendula flowers, lemon verbena, cinnamon, cloves, orris root powder and essential oils. We would pick these fragrant ingredients on balmy, bee-laden days. Then Dad dried the harvest and brought it together to make the potpourri in a veritable act of alchemy. It saddens me now to see how the notion of a potpourri has become debased. These days, it is often just another commercial room freshener, redolent with sickly artificial scents, or an extremely bad imitation of the original concept made of poor quality dried leaves and coloured wood shavings. I emerged from my reverie when we saw some women nimbly gathering the delicate blooms and carrying them in large baskets on their heads, each moving with a gliding elegance.

The next village we drove through was where Satish had grown up, its streets barely wide enough to accommodate the bus. One could have reached out the windows and touched the shops and stalls as we drove past them. Every aspect of village life was going on around us: merchants selling their wares, tailors sewing, men lazily drinking coffee and smoking or urinating against walls, children scampering around like little jackrabbits. The bus strained up a steep rise, chugged around a sharp bend in the road, then stopped at the local police post. Satish got out and for about five minutes was engaged in heated conversation with the moustached, baton-under-the-arm officer. Some money changed hands, Satish climbed back on board and we were on our way again.

The road began to get bumpier and occasionally we

heard some alarming knocks and clunks in the bus's suspension and imagined what it would be like to have a broken axle or tailshaft out here. Our attention was drawn away from this prospect when we came upon some enormous brick structures that we discovered were traditional brickworks. Like so many experiences in this country, we could have been in a time warp from centuries ago. The people working here were not locals, but comprised about twenty families from Orissa, approximately a thousand kilometres to the north-east, between Andhra Pradesh and Bengal. Amongst the workers were about ten Gypsy women wearing an abundance of ornate silver bands on their arms and legs, brightly coloured clothes and more silver ornaments braided into their hair. They spontaneously formed a circle around us and performed a beautiful rhythmic dance accompanied by singing. The other workers gathered around to watch until the boss came over and hurried them all back to work. We felt we'd been lucky to experience something so welcoming and uncontrived, the Gypsies sharing some of their culture for the pure joy of it. Satish told us these workers need to make about 750 bricks to earn the equivalent of one dollar; hard work indeed, especially when one sees a woman carrying ten bricks on her head.

The kiln, which has been made in a similar fashion for centuries, is basically a huge stack of bricks piled up to 10 metres high, 50 metres long and 20 metres wide. A firebox set inside the stack, aspirated by vents left open during the construction, burns for weeks until the whole structure is baked. Then it is dismantled and the bricks are sold.

The road deteriorated even further and we drove at about 10 kilometres an hour until we reached the small village of Kodlapadkal, a remote settlement where we were told no other tourists had been before. The only westerners to visit in the last ten years had been some research workers with the United Nations. All the houses were made of mud with thatched roofs and had dirt alleys running between them. We received a warm and friendly welcome, although there was curiosity on both sides. For us their way of life appeared nothing short of idyllic – making pots, weaving matting, with children playing and old people chatting. The villagers entertained us and we them for an hour and a half until we had to go. Everyone was quiet on the bus, just cherishing our experience and hoping that as civilisation encroaches upon this remote area, the inhabitants benefit from the good aspects of progress and are not demeaned by the greedy, bad and ugly.

The bus pulled up beside a huge tamarind tree (*Tamarindus indica*), and we laid out the enormous red rugs on the ground under the shade of its spreading branches. There is a belief that tamarind trees emit harmful, acrid vapours, making it unsafe to sleep under them, and that plants will not grow there because of the acidity exhaled from the tree overnight. This may be why there is usually little vegetation around their base, creating an ideal picnic spot in the middle of a hot Indian March day.

The hour or so spent over the very un-Indian, hotel-packed lunch of sandwiches, fresh fruit and hard-boiled eggs, passed with relaxed conversation and some hilarity. We wanted to thank the villagers of Kodlapadkal for their hospitality, so after consultation with Satish, we passed the hat around and made a donation to a fund that had been established to install a pump for their well.

Just four days out of Hyderabad, our next stop was Ahmedabad, 600 kilometres north-west of Mumbai and the closest we came to the Pakistan border.

At that time of year, before the monsoon season begins in July, Ahmedabad was a dustbowl with so much air pollution that we kept the windows of the bus closed in spite of the heat. In stark contrast to our earlier subtropical adventures, we were surrounded by a dry, undulating landscape, reminiscent of Australia's wheat belt. Perfect conditions for seed crops. I can never doze on a bus because I worry that I might miss something, such as the things I saw this day — a cart piled precariously high with a haystack of mustard straw and pulled by an equally straw-coloured, haughty-looking camel, or a group of women in bright saris, with colours like bougainvillea flowers against the colourless background, working on road repairs.

The roads were as congested as any we had seen. The driver would frantically toot and weave his way through a tangle of pushcarts, camel and oxen-drawn drays and light three-wheeler auto-rickshaws stacked high with goods. Every now and then we'd inch past lumbering, suspension-challenged Tata trucks that look just like 1950s Mercedes trucks, but bear a large 'T' on the bonnet instead of a three-pointed star.

Something a group of tourists has to come to terms with in India is that not every city has a five-star hotel. When we arrived at the hotel we had booked, reputed to be the best in town, Liz and I saw a few jaws drop. It was characterised by flaking paint, mould marks on the walls, uneven floors, and doors and door jambs that had seen far better days. The beds were chiropractically firm, yet it was good to discover how impeccably clean the bathrooms were. What endeared the hotel to us, though, was the hospitality of the management and their efforts to make us comfortable. The chef had found out where we had come from and knowing that Australia had been a colony of England went to great lengths to provide a meal of fish and chips followed by boiled pudding and custard. We appreciated his kindness but wished he'd served the food he prepares every day. Although the fish and chips left a lot to be desired (the oil that is ideal for Indian cooking is probably not the most appropriate to fry up fish and chips), the boiled pudding was fabulous. The next day we were treated to steak and mushroom pie followed by non-alcoholic trifle; Gujarat is a 'dry' state. India has a number of states governed by Muslims where alcohol is not allowed. No doubt our brain cells appreciated a few days respite from us slaking our thirsts with large amber bottles of cold Kingfisher beer in the 'wet' states.

We had made sure everyone was comfortable for the night, arranged wake-up calls for the morning and discussed the next day's itinerary with Dr Mehta, a specialist in spices from the agricultural university at Jagadon. No sooner were we asleep than, close to midnight, we heard the most incredible commotion in the street outside. Guns were going off, shouting and screams were punctuating the air, and the percussion of sticks on tin reverberated through our flaking walls. The Gulf War was not long past and the general feeling of anxiety while travelling at this time was probably more heightened than usual. 'Bloody hell,' I said to Liz as I shot bolt upright in bed. 'What on earth's going on? Has World War Three started? What about our group?' We sprang out of bed, tentatively pulling the curtains aside, peering out so as not to be seen by the rioting mob, and expected to be confronted with a scene of bloody devastation. Instead, in the street below we saw a group of about fifty revellers, including a line of young women beautifully dressed in red and gold saris. The cause of so much hubbub was a wedding procession.

Dr Mehta met us early next morning to take us to the Spices Research Station and we hoped to have time to see the spice market town of Unja in the afternoon. Dr Mehta was a short, neat man with a pencil-thin moustache. He wore thick-lensed, black-framed spectacles, navy trousers and leather sandals and despite this hot and dusty environment, his spotlessly white shirt was impeccable and freshly ironed. Dr Mehta had hosted an Australian from the South Australian Seed Growers' Co-operative (SEEDCO) a few days earlier, and having developed somewhat of a rapport with one of our countrymen, he felt very much at ease with our group. The visitor was on a study tour because SEEDCO had developed a substantial industry growing coriander seed in its wheat-producing areas and was keen to exchange information with the Indian growers. Instead of harvesting by hand, Australia's coriander seed crop is harvested with wheat headers, making production in a country with high labour costs economically viable. Unfortunately the visitor from South Australia had been a little too adventurous with his choice of eating establishments and had succumbed to a major dose of 'Delhi belly', which cut short his stay. We prayed no such fate would befall us.

The great thing about India is that in the same way Australia has a Wheat Board and a Wool Board, it has a Spices Board. A government body, the Spices Board of India is actively involved in assisting with all aspects of the spice trade, from growing and harvesting, to processing and marketing Indian spices. An important part of this involvement is research, conducted at a number of locations in spice-producing areas. Dr Thampi (who was Mr Thampi then, and the publicity officer) arranged for us to visit their facility in Ahmedabad.

As we approached the Spices Research Station the earthy aroma of cumin, tinged with the smell of wood smoke from cooking fires, was in the air. On our arrival we were shown a display of spices complete with statistics that I lapped up while the rest of the group politely showed interest that did not quite match my own. Seed spices represent about 10 per cent of India's export of spices, which by 1991 was approaching 90,000 tonnes. Dr Mehta explained how their research focused on three main areas – crop improvement, agronomics and plant protection.

Crop improvement comes first, because as any farmer knows the search for varieties that are robust, high yielding and practical to harvest is never-ending. Agronomics relates to planting methods, timing and general plant husbandry, which will lead to high productivity. All this work can be rendered useless if the crops are then attacked by pests or diseases. Plant protection is another essential aspect in their research, which we were impressed to learn included organic farming methods. Organic farming, or farming without chemicals, has begun to gain some attention in India over recent years. This is because some shipments of produce had been rejected by European and

North American buyers due to chemical residues. What really got up the growers' noses was that the countries rejecting the goods were the very same nations that had been selling the chemicals to them in the first place.

In India many crops, and spices in particular, are cultivated on small family-run holdings that may be less than one hectare in size. For this reason Dr Mehta and his field officers have to conduct their research in a manner that is relative to the small farmer. There is no point in coming up with high-technology solutions that no one would have the resources to implement. The field officers go out to the farmers and painstakingly explain and demonstrate the most basic and useful methods that will help them continue to improve the quality and yield of their crops. For example, some cultivars (different strains within a species) that bear more seeds per plant will increase the yield per hectare. Drying the harvested seed heads in a shaded area, no matter how crudely constructed, instead of in the sun, will produce better looking, more flavoursome seeds.

Soon it was time to stride out among the orderly rows of trial plantings. Coriander plants grown for a maximum yield of seeds and looking straggly and lean compared to the lush plants at home, beckoned us with their seed-laden umbels. Members of this family of plants were once referred to as *Umbelliferae* because the seeds are borne in umbrella-shaped flower-heads.

Botanical names provide a system of plant classification that is universally accepted. The first attempt at classifying plants was made by Theophrastus in the fourth century BC. Theophrastus classified plants as either herbs, shrubs or trees. At that time 'herb' was merely a reference to the plant size, rather than an indication of any culinary or medicinal attributes, which tend to be the basis today. Carl Linnaeus made the next significant and enduring step in 1753, when his writings in *Species Plantatum* noted differences in the form of flowers. The drawback with this method is that it relies on grouping plants that share one particular characteristic. This does not necessarily indicate the true genetic commonality with other similar plants. Therefore in recent times many botanical and family names have been changed and the family *Umbelliferae* is now referred to as *Apiaceae*. We saw plots where fourteen different varieties of coriander (*Coriandrum sativum*) were grown. We also saw rudimentary drying frames, shaded with thatch to let the air flow freely and dry the hanging bunches of seeds, protected from sunlight that bleaches out colour and causes loss of flavour.

The task of drying herbs and spices can be very involved and there is usually much more to it than just putting them out in the sun to dry. Drying, or dehydration as we call it in the trade, is the process whereby most of the moisture is removed while retaining the volatile oils that give the herb or spice its flavour. When it is dried a herb will have a moisture content of between 10 and 12 per cent, as opposed to over 80 per cent when it is fresh. The low moisture level then acts as a preservative, because without water mould and other bacteria that would rot the vegetative matter cannot survive. The challenge, whether drying fennel seeds, chillies or fenugreek leaves, is to remove the moisture at the right pace. Too slow and mould will start growing before it is dry, too fast and the heat used to dry the plant quickly will drive off the volatile oils and destroy the flavour. Every herb or spice will behave differently. Chillies have a thick, glossy skin that keeps moisture in, while parsley leaves readily let go of their water content, making drying in a dark place with the application of a little heat dead easy.

I remember my father making a drying rack for herbs that was very effective. In our roadside shop at Dural, north-west of Sydney, Dad would dry various herbs to pack into bottles and sell, or use in making potpourri. He made the drying rack by constructing a frame, which was 4 metres long, 2 metres wide and about 200 millimetres deep. Flyscreen netting was stretched across the bottom of the frame so air could circulate freely around the herbs as they dried. The really ingenious, yet simple, idea that made this work so well was a system of ropes attached to each corner of the frame. These ropes were fed through pulleys attached to the shop ceiling, so like a canvas blind, when the ropes were pulled down the frame would come up. When it was full of leaves Dad would 'raise the boom', taking the cargo up close to the ceiling where it was dark and warm. Hot air rises and in this dark, warm environment the herbs dried perfectly. To check them, Dad would 'clear the decks and lower the boom', and if crisp and dry, another harvest would be raked up with a little wooden croupier's shovel he had made from plywood.

After leaving the coriander, we strolled through waist-high drifts of white ajowan flowers (*Trachyspermum amni*), a plant often referred to as bishop's weed that produces tiny brown seeds. Ajowan is a great source of thymol, a volatile oil also found in thyme, which has been used for centuries to relieve coughs and congestion. Until the early twentieth century, almost all India's production of ajowan seeds was sent to Germany for the distillation and extraction of the oil thymol. The savoury flavour of these seeds is delicious in vegetable and seafood curries.

Liz lost sight of me when I disappeared into a stand of fennel (*Foeniculum vulgare*). The plants' exotic, high-yielding flowers were covered with cloth to prevent cross-pollination with other varieties. In the warming sun, the sounds of bees, and the aroma of crushed foliage as I pushed through row upon row of seed spices, reminded me of a childhood spent among herbs and their fragrances. That must be why I felt so comfortable in this environment.

I was delighted to find fenugreek (*Trigonella foenum-graecum*) ready to harvest. Its common names, 'goat's horn' and 'cow's horn', refer to the horn-like shape of its seed pod, which looks like a miniature broad bean and contains ten to twenty hard, light brown seeds. These seeds smell of green peas. No wonder, because it belongs to the same family as beans and peas, and has a sharp sweetness like maple syrup. I was not surprised to learn that an extract of fenugreek seeds is used to make imitation maple syrup. Next time you smell some fenugreek seeds, shut your eyes, inhale and think of maple syrup – you'll be amazed. Many cooks will tell you to dry-roast fenugreek seeds in a hot pan if you are using them in a curry. This is a good idea, but be careful not to over-roast them as the taste will become bitter and unpalatable. Fenugreek leaves are also used in Indian cooking to impart a 'beany' flavour with less sharpness and bitterness than the seeds. When the leaves are used they are generally referred to as 'methi'.

The aroma of cumin (*Cuminum cyminum*) was still lingering in the air, and as we walked towards a lean-to shelter with a swept concrete apron within the Research Station we realised why. A group of women in colourful saris were winnowing the 2 millimetre tails from the rubbed seeds. Cumin seeds are pale brown to khaki in colour and have a downy surface, which gives them a dull appearance. Each seed has a fine, hair-like tail and the women were rubbing the seeds across the palms of their hands to remove this tail, then letting handfuls fall past a primitive fan that blew the fine particles away as the seeds fell to the ground. Dr Mehta beckoned to me as I was about to plunge into a row of yellow-flowered dill plants (*Anethum sowa*) and said that we had better move on if we were to get to Unja and see more spices. See more spices, how could I resist?

From the bus windows we spotted an oxen pulling a cart around in a circle over what looked like a big pile of straw. When we got closer, we saw the beast and its driver were threshing brown mustard seeds (*Brassica juncea*). The mustard had been harvested when the seed-bearing pods were fully developed but not yet ripe. This is done because ripe pods will shatter during gathering and many seeds would be lost. After cutting, the mustard hay is stacked in sheaves to dry, then threshed by simply laying it on the ground and driving an ox-cart over the pile to break the pods and release the seeds. Off to one side three young men standing in a calf-deep pile of shiny, brown mustard seeds were shaking an enormous sieve, about 2 metres in diameter, while another worker loaded more trampled hay onto it. Although these seeds are brown, they are often called black mustard seeds. This is because there is another variety named *Brassica nigra* (which is, strictly speaking, the true black mustard seed) that looks identical to *Brassica juncea* and has a slightly stronger flavour, but its seed pods shatter very easily, making it difficult to harvest and so less popular as a commercial crop.

Over the next rise we were treated to a scene I had not

even been game to hope for. An area the size of two football fields stretched out before us, covered in bright red chillies (*Capsicum annum*) drying in the sun. Hundreds of growers were bringing their produce of ripe, fiery chillies from their tiny plots and selling them to the buyer who was drying and preparing them for the market. The variety grown in this area is long and thin and called *rasham patta*. We noticed a fellow sitting on the ground with a pile of chillies in front of him. His job was to remove the stems from the chillies in that pile, then move on to another lot and de-stem them. After their stems were removed the chillies were laid out on the ground to dry and cure in the sun. Curing, or slow-drying, is an important element in chilli production as it concentrates the colour and helps to develop the flavour. Some people don't realise that a dried chilli has a very different flavour from a fresh one. A bit like the difference between a fresh tomato and a sun-dried one, the sugars in chillies caramelise during drying and create a rich, robust and complex flavour. For this reason, most Indian recipes will use dried chilli in preference to fresh. Gazing at this immense area of chillies drying out in the sun, we asked the foreman, 'What do you do if it rains?' He replied in a tone of unswerving confidence, 'It won't rain until the fourteenth of April.' Liz thought there was a definite opening in Australia for him as a weather forecaster.

These chillies were destined, as we were, for the market town of Unja, or as I would like to call it, 'Spice Heaven'. It's a town dedicated to chillies, turmeric and garlic, where whole roads and alleys are lined with warehouses brimming with hessian bags bursting at the seams as if the chillies were trying to escape from their twine bonds. The aroma of chilli and its hot, sinus-clearing, throat-searing substance called capsaicin, permeated the air. Everyone in the group coughed, gasped and wheezed and hightailed it back to the bus leaving Andrew (a spice trader from Brisbane who had joined our tour), Liz and me to continue exploring this Aladdin's cave of laneways, godowns and old-fashioned, one-tonne, beam-balance scales. Workers in bare feet with sarongs around their waists carried huge bags of chillies over their shoulders, seemingly oblivious to the eye-watering, skin-irritating effects of their loads. I could not help but imagine that I had travelled back in time and was in Ahmedabad in the 1620s, when trade with the British East India Company was in its heyday. As it must have been then, all around me was a hive of bustling industry and commerce, shouts of bargaining and the cursing of idle labourers, punctuated by the clunking thuds of overladen drays traversing rutted streets.

We departed this part of India with a very different perspective from the first impressions we'd had when we arrived in Ahmedabad. The region which had initially seemed so dry, dusty and smoky, turned out to be a landscape dotted with diversity. The dedication and passion of people such as Dr Mehta and the work performed at such a basic level by the Indian Spices Board left us humbled and hopeful that these people will achieve their goals in an increasingly complex and technological world.

In the FOOTSTEPS
of the CONQUISTADORS

One can only imagine how the Spaniard Hernan Cortés must have felt as he experienced his first taste of vanilla and chocolate in 1520 when the Aztec emperor Montezuma treated him to an exotic chocolate and vanilla drink sweetened with honey. So impressed were the Spanish with this discovery that production was established in Spain for the manufacture of chocolate, flavoured with vanilla, which was imported from Mexico. Sadly for Montezuma, he not only disclosed his secret beverage, but Cortés plundered his empire and had him executed. The vanilla-flavoured chocolate industry thrived in Europe and the consumption of its product became an obsession for a considerable percentage of the world's population.

The nuances of vanilla, its origins and the magical transformation that turns a bland green bean into an extraordinary taste sensation, fascinated me. I had read about vanilla and how it comes from a tropical flowering orchid, the genus of which happens to be the largest family of flowering plants in the world, encompassing some twenty thousand species. And I'd heard about the legendary powers attributed to the vanilla bean. But I wanted to learn more.

As it turned out, my curiosity was to be satisfied. I was scheduled to attend a conference in London, and it seemed an excellent idea for Liz and me to travel via the United States and Mexico so we could actually see a vanilla plantation. We wanted to discover for ourselves the growing habits, processing techniques and the unique character of this spice referred to as *vainilla* in Mexico, which means 'little scabbard' in Spanish.

The first challenge was to find a vanilla producer we could visit, and then work out exactly how to get there. A business contact in Queretaro put us in touch with Señor Jose Gonzalez Miaja, a vanilla trader in Papantla, which lies a little over 200 kilometres north-east of Mexico City. Señor Gonzalez arranged to meet us at Poza Rica, a short flight east of Mexico City, and take us to a vanilla plantation and processor on Mexico's eastern slopes, which descend to the Gulf of Mexico.

This was our first visit to Mexico City and we were a little concerned about our ability to find our way around a city of 22 million people, and us speaking no Spanish. The start did not augur well; the taxi took us to the wrong hotel, which had a similar name to the one we had booked. The consolation was to drive in one of the many old-style VW beetle taxis to the correct hotel. This trip provided ample proof of the benefits of travelling light; less is distinctly more convenient in practically every imaginable travel situation.

Our flight to the east was a day away, so we decided to visit the archaeological site of Teotihuacan, 40 kilometres to the north-east of Mexico City. Famed for its pyramids, the city was inhabited from 100 BC to AD 700 and had systems for collecting rain and using underground water. Evidence remains of artisans' workshops, markets, streets, temples and palaces. We tried to imagine what life must have been like here around 2000 years ago, as we stood on the 40 metre wide road known as the Avenue of the Dead. In front of us was the imposing 60 metre high Pyramid of the Sun, the Pyramid of the Moon was to our left and the Temple of Quetzalcoatl on the other side of the tiny San Juan River, further down to our right. A considerable amount of reconstruction has been undertaken and to show what has been rebuilt, pebbles are dotted in the mortar of the new work. Although there are many theories as to why Teotihuacan was abandoned by the eighth century, the precise reason for its decline remains a mystery.

Like so many tourists, I could not resist climbing the seemingly endless rows of stone steps to the top of the Pyramid of the Sun. The unusually high steps made me feel Lilliputian. Were the builders of these pyramids giants with abnormally long legs? Perhaps, as for me, the sense of achievement at reaching the top was designed to feel all the greater, or such effort was meant to be a humbling experience. On this warm October day the panoramic view from the summit was uncharacteristically clear, the smog of Mexico City far away. A cool breeze offered some relief after the climb and by the time I met Liz halfway down (she had the sense to be satisfied with the view halfway up) my thigh and calf muscles were groaning in anguish from making that extra stretch with every step up. We spent many hours wandering around, marvelling at the civilisations that existed thousands of years ago.

Later that afternoon we took in a supermarket. Nothing tells you more about the way the majority of people in a society eat and drink than their shops or markets. In the case of Mexico City we wandered through a huge Aurrera supermarket, more of a hypermarket, it was so big. The first thing that struck us was the bright yellow of the fresh chicken carcasses. Apparently in Mexico, a good quality corn-fed chicken will have yellow flesh. To enhance this appearance the processed birds are often artificially coloured. A popular colouring agent is made from annatto seed (*Bixa orellana*), a small, pyramid-shaped seed that has a dark, red-oxide-coloured surface. Annatto is native to this region but is now grown in many tropical countries. Its fresh seeds have such a bright red coating that the tree is often referred to as the 'lipstick tree'. Annatto is the main ingredient in *achiote* paste, a spicy garlic, cumin and oregano marinade for chicken. These days many naturally coloured processed foods, such as margarine, use natural colour E1606 made from annatto.

The range of spices on display in the supermarket was similar to what one would see in many developed countries, except for the huge range of chillies, most of them dried. In contrast to the relatively hot, red chillies we had seen in India, here we saw a wide variety of dark purple, almost black dried chillies. Among these varieties we saw *ancho*, *pasilla* (pronounced paa-see-ya) and *mulato*. An enormous deep red chilli – some up to 20 centimetres long – was the fruity 'New Mexico' variety. These chillies are not terribly hot – I rate them between three and five on a heat scale that has ten as the hottest – and they are surprisingly meaty in taste. When you break these dark chillies open and smell them, you are reminded of dried fruits with notes of coffee, tobacco, wood and raisins. We flavour casseroles with them. The best method is to soak a dried chilli in hot water for ten to twenty minutes, remove the stem and scrape out the seeds, chop up the soft flesh and add at the start of cooking. Don't throw the water away; either add it to the dish or keep it in the refrigerator to use as a spicy stock the next time stock is required in a recipe. This chilli water makes a good vegetarian substitute for beef stock.

The following morning we had an early start and took a taxi, this time a more comfortable old Chevrolet, to the *aeropuerto* for our flight to Poza Rica. As the small plane carrying fewer than thirty passengers took off, we could see the Sun and Moon pyramids at Teotihuacan from the air. The flight took us over lush mountains and plateaus until we reached the utilitarian, shed-like airport at Poza Rica. On our arrival we were greeted by the vanilla traders, Señor Jose Gonzalez Miaja and his daughter Marguerite. Señor Jose, as we learnt to call him, was prosperous looking, urbane, well rounded (his wide leather belt stretched around his white trousers) and spoke no English. Luckily for us, Marguerite spoke English very well, and as we climbed into Señor Jose's enormous Chevrolet Suburban station wagon, she cut straight to the chase. She produced samples of about five different grades of vanilla beans, which Liz and I smelt, fondled, rolled between thumb and forefinger and generally admired.

Much to our surprise, Marguerite told us we were lucky to have missed the earthquake. Apparently there had been a small one near Mexico City while we were in the air and about thirty people had been killed. We found the news somewhat chilling, and a phone call back to our family in Australia became the priority that evening. No matter how far loved ones are from a disaster that occurs in the country they are travelling in, those at home tend to expect the worst when they hear of it. We are the same when our grown-up daughters are overseas.

Señor Jose drove us through the rich, tropical landscape that we were told is typical of the Mexican state of Vera Cruz, positioned on the western side of the Gulf of Mexico, looking east towards the Yucatan Peninsula. A little over an hour's drive led us to a rough track that the Chevy, with its high ground clearance, negotiated with ease. Eventually we stopped at the gate of a vanilla farm, which to the uninitiated would look like just another patch of tropical rainforest, in the picturesque valley of Zamora. The air was heavy with humidity and filled with the buzz of insects. We walked along a narrow track, soft and spongy underfoot from years of accumulated humus, and coloured deep red-brown by the combination of compost and rich, volcanic soil. It smelled of cloying tropical vegetation and was so dark I began to wonder if my 400ASA film would be sufficiently fast, in the low light, to capture the quarry we had come in search of.

To our excitement, Marguerite pointed out that we were surrounded by vanilla vines, their succulent stems clinging to host trees by long, dry, brown aerial roots. The leaves were flat, large and fleshy, rounded at the stem and tapering to a cow-lick pointed tip. Vanilla vines will grow on any host tree but are not parasitic. Farmers prefer to grow them on small trees so the vine does not grow out of reach for pollination and harvesting.

When vines that have reached the top of the tree hang down, the farmers loop them up again like elegant, green curtain cords to maintain easy access.

In their natural habitat vanilla flowers were pollinated by tiny bees of the *Melapona* genus. However these bees are almost extinct, so every vanilla flower has to be pollinated by hand if a bean is to be produced. To complicate matters further, there is a small membrane in the flower that prevents the stigma (the female organ of the flower) and stamen (the male organ) from naturally touching and pollinating. Hand pollination of these mildly fragrant, pale green flowers is painstaking. The flower is only open for eight hours and during that time the farmer must find every open flower, then with a small implement like a toothpick, move the membrane aside and touch the stigma and stamen together. *Voilà*, pollination! But only about 50 per cent of those flowers pollinated will produce beans (or pods as they are sometimes called when still on the vine). About six weeks after successful fertilisation, the pods will appear and will mature for six to nine months into fully grown beans, ranging in length from 10 to 20 centimetres. There is little change in the appearance of the beans between six and nine months. If the shrivelled flower is still attached, the beans will continue to grow plumper until the flower eventually falls off. A good farmer will go through the plantation and remove curved and crooked pods, retaining the vine's vital energy to develop the straightest, best-looking pods, which are most sought after as 'gourmet-grade' whole beans. Marguerite told us that it takes farmers two days to pick about 300 kilograms of beans – not a great deal compared to most agricultural crops – from one hectare.

You can imagine our horror when Señor Jose, via Marguerite, told us that one of the biggest problems they have is *bandidos* poaching the beans just before harvest and selling them on the black market. In the old days farmers would brand each bean like ranchers brand cattle. This was done by placing rows of pins in a cork to form a pattern. The green beans would then be 'branded' while still on the vine and the brand identifying the farm the beans came from would be visible after curing. These days the problem of thieving has been reduced by a government regulation that states vanilla beans can only be traded after the official close of harvest. This has been successful in preventing robbers from undercutting legitimate growers by selling vanilla that was stolen before the beans had matured on the vine. On this subject Señor Jose informed us that the Indonesians pick their beans at five months, as compared with the Mexican maturing period of nine months, to foil poachers. For this reason the Indonesian vanilla is not as good as Mexican.

We marvelled how the Aztecs had fathomed that a green tasteless bean could transform into a culinary delight when it was cured, and the answer lay at our feet on the forest floor. Some beans that had fallen to the ground had cured naturally, and although not as strongly flavoured as a properly cured bean, here was a sweet, almost black, soft and pliable, semi-cured vanilla bean. My mind flashed to a probable scene thousands of years ago. I could imagine a partially cured bean being picked up by a small child or a toothless granny and sucked on with great delight. How the discovery was really made is immaterial, the exciting thing for us was that we were about to learn how this process has evolved into one of the most interesting in the world of flavour.

We drove towards the Gaya processing factory in Gutierrez in the Zamora area of Vera Cruz. The Gaya family has been processing vanilla exclusively from native plants since 1875 and claims to be the oldest company processing vanilla in Mexico. As the harvest was still some months away, the small town with its narrow streets and whitewashed buildings felt incredibly quiet. Contributing to this atmosphere of inactivity was the late morning warmth that had begun to usher the villagers inside behind thick adobe walls, to prepare for lunch, followed by a traditional siesta. The Gaya factory, which is a hive of activity during the curing season, had a ghost-like emptiness at this time of year. The timber drying racks, fourteen tiers high and stained by years of contact with rich, sticky vanilla beans, looked like the surreal masts of sailing ships.

The first step in the vanilla curing process is referred to as 'killing', or wilting the beans, to stop further development in the fresh bean and initiate the enzyme reaction that creates the character of vanilla. In the Mexican process, this is achieved when the freshly harvested beans are heated for about forty-eight hours in a wood-fired kiln that becomes no hotter than 70 degrees centigrade. It is also common in some vanilla-producing areas such as Madagascar to achieve 'killing' by first plunging the beans into boiling water. This process is referred to as the 'Bourbon' method, first developed on the French island of Reunion, formerly known as Bourbon.

The next steps are 'sunning' and 'sweating', their purpose being to accelerate the enzyme reaction that creates the flavour of vanilla. An enzyme is a protein produced by living cells and it functions as a catalyst in a biochemical reaction. The magic of enzymes is particularly important in the world of spices, for without them pepper would not turn black when dried, cloves would lack their distinctive flavour and mustard would never be hot.

Back to the process at the Gaya factory – the green beans are packed into little wooden crates which measure about 40 centimetres long by 20 centimetres wide and are as deep as they are wide. These crates are then stacked four high on shelves in one of the three kilns, which are each about the size of a small bedroom (about 4 metres square). Marguerite mentioned that although attempts have been made to modernise this process, vanilla cured any other way does not have the same flavour. I couldn't help wondering whether the wood-fired kiln, which must impart some smoky flavour notes to the curing beans, was not a key element in the chain of traditional processes that creates the distinct profile of Mexican vanilla.

If you thought a lot of work had gone into getting the vanilla to this stage, the time and effort to produce great vanilla was only just starting. After two days in the kiln the beans are laid out on woollen blankets in the sunshine (sunning) in an enormous courtyard with 2 metre high whitewashed walls, no doubt to keep the troublesome *bandidos* at bay. During the middle of the day the blackening beans absorb the heat of the sun, so much so that they can be almost too hot to handle by mid afternoon. In the evening the beans are taken inside, stacked on the high racks in large wooden bins or wrapped in blankets or straw, where they will sweat (sweating) overnight. The next day they will be taken outside again to absorb more heat in the scorching Mexican sun. That night they are once again brought inside. This process continues for up to thirty days on a rotational basis. The head vanilla curer monitors each batch and determines how long each one should spend in the sun, and what period of time under shelter, sweating.

The third stage involves slow-drying at normal temperatures on the racks inside until the beans have lost about two-thirds of their original weight. The cured beans are then sorted and graded according to their quality, which is determined by two main criteria – vanillin content and appearance. Beans destined for the culinary bean market have to look straight, plump and uniform in addition to possessing superior flavour. Beans used for making vanilla extract must have similar flavour attributes, however appearance is not so important.

The fourth and final stage is known as 'conditioning'. This is when the pliable beans are graded and tied into bundles of approximately one hundred and stored in boxes for up to three months to fully develop their desired aroma and flavour. Few experiences are as conducive to swooning as the first time you handle one of these highly aromatic, sensuous bundles. A bundle of a hundred gourmet-grade vanilla beans weighs about 500 grams. It is tied at each end and in the middle with black twine so tightly applied that the soft beans crease. The strapped beans are perfectly uniform, oily to touch, heavy and highly aromatic.

By the time the beans have been fully cured and the enzymes have completed their task of creating vanillin, the substance that gives vanilla its flavour and aroma, a bean may have been handled anywhere between 100 and 250 times. What's more, it takes 5 kilograms of freshly harvested green pods to produce just 1 kilogram of shiny, black vanilla beans.

We were fortunate that although the curing was not in progress at this time of year, vanilla extract was being made in another section of the factory that is adjacent to a little shop that sells Gaya products. Vanilla extract is made by first chopping cured vanilla beans in a machine that looks a bit like a large washing machine with blades instead of paddles. More than 30 kilograms of this chopped vanilla is then placed in a 200 litre stainless-steel extractor, where an alcohol and water solution extracts the vanilla flavour from the macerated beans over a period of about 100 hours. This natural vanilla extract is vastly superior to the artificial vanilla essences which are made as by-products of the paper or petro-chemical industries.

Our hosts took some delight in explaining how one type of artificial vanilla is made by extracting the sulphite solutions that are derived during the process of cleaning wood for use in paper manufacture. The sulphite solutions are continually processed until the artificial vanilla extractive is produced. The final product is called lignin vanillin and is certainly less appetising to our palates than the real thing.

Pure vanilla is a complex flavour that contains some 300 naturally occurring flavour compounds, and try as they have, flavour scientists have never been able to duplicate the unique flavour and aroma characteristics of real vanilla. You might also see some so-called 'thick' vanilla essences, but these may not be all that they appear as the thickness is usually created by the addition of sugar, glycerine, propylene glycol (anti-freeze) and dextrose or corn syrup. It always pays to read the ingredients list on the label closely so you know what you are getting. Depending upon the packaging laws in the country you are in, true vanilla is usually labelled 'natural vanilla extract' with some reference to the alcohol content such as 'less than 35 per cent by volume'. I am often asked what the difference is between an essence and an extract. An extract is made by extracting the desired attributes of a substance. Soaking vanilla in alcohol extracts the vanilla flavour. An essence is either a distilled or concentrated extract, or an artificial copy of the distinctive characteristic attributes of a substance. This explains why artificial vanilla is generally labelled 'imitation vanilla essence'.

We discovered how truly delicious real vanilla is when we were treated to a glass of Gaya's Vanilla Liqueur Xanath, an alcoholic liqueur reminiscent of Tia Maria but tasting of wood smoke and rich vanilla. The liqueur seemed to go straight to our heads. We had not eaten since leaving Mexico City that morning and the midday sun, combined with the excitement of the morning's discoveries was a sure recipe for narcosis. Liz then spotted a curiosity on sale. There were shelves of plaited shapes and figures made entirely from vanilla beans. One was a heart about 6 centimetres high with an arrow through it, another a flower, and there were even dolls and a perfectly woven small basket, large enough to hold an apple. They were all plaited from freshly cured, pliable beans by nimble-fingered women in the village. Liz was so impressed that a couple of years later, when we'd opened our shop, she ordered some. We went to great lengths to get a Spanish interpreter, remembering that the Gayas spoke no English. The interpreter helped us with faxes to and fro when we placed our first order for vanilla beans, extract and these little figures. In our naivety we ordered twenty *Chico Christo*, expecting that they might be a little simple crucifix shape. When the shipment arrived we opened the soldered tin to much hilarity when we discovered that they were beautifully plaited little crosses about 12 centimetres high with a body of Christ attached to them. We decided that it would not be in good taste to sell them at Easter time, so Liz duly undid the intricate plaiting and we had these formerly religious vanilla pieces flavouring our plunger coffee for months to come.

On that note, vanilla complements coffee beautifully. The best way to flavour it is to put about one-third of a bean, for four cups, cut into 5 millimetre bits, into the plunger with the coffee grounds. Pour in the hot water (never boiling as water that is too hot will destroy the volatile top notes of the vanilla and the coffee) and enjoy.

There are a couple of popular ways to use vanilla in everyday cooking. You may have seen vanilla ice-cream or a vanilla-flavoured thick cream with thousands of tiny black specks through it. These specks are actually the seeds that are contained in the black, sticky mass found inside a plump, cured vanilla bean, and they are like concentrated vanilla when you use them. The easiest way to remove the gooey seeds is to slit the bean lengthwise with a sharp knife, lay it open and then scrape out the sticky mass binding the seeds. We always get the best results when we have mixed them through the cream (unflavoured yoghurt is also delicious) a few hours or even overnight before serving. This way the flavour has a chance to fully infuse and work its magic. When you have scraped out a vanilla bean in this way, never discard the skin as it still retains a lot of useful flavour. You can even put a 'has bean' in the caster sugar canister, then you'll have vanilla-flavoured sugar on hand when making cakes and biscuits.

You can infuse a whole vanilla bean when you want the flavour, but don't want the little black specks through the dish.

If you are poaching pears in Champagne for breakfast (the sort of thing we would love to do more often), put a whole vanilla bean in with the fruit and sugar syrup while it is simmering. When cooked, take out the bean, wash it under warm water and slip it into the sugar canister until it is required. You can use a vanilla bean two to three times this way and each time it will yield its heavenly taste. The rules are a little different if the vanilla bean has been infused in milk (say for custard), as any protein from the milk may go off. It is best to wrap these beans in cling-wrap and keep them in the refrigerator until needed. Properly cured vanilla beans are best stored in the coolest part of the kitchen in an airtight pack. Don't keep them in the refrigerator or freezer because I have heard from the Gayas and other vanilla experts that this will damage the flavour.

Liz and I allowed ourselves to be plied with a little more Vanilla Liqueur Xanath until Señor Jose suggested it was almost time we had some lunch. We drove down to the coast through lush vegetation until we reached a restaurant named Hotel el Palmar on Costa Smeralda, the 55 kilometre beach on the Gulf of Mexico. Lunch was simple and not what we expected. Fish cutlets poached in a cream and chilli sauce washed down with some Corona beer. What a tough life, we thought, drinking Corona on the Costa Smeralda and enjoying the company of our hosts, even though Marguerite was the only one we really understood. We love to travel on business but we often wonder what it would be like to slow down a little, spend a few days or more in an idyllic location like this and really get to know a place. Even better, how wonderful to be able to stay long enough to experience every part of the life-cycle of a spice from pollination to the final product. That is one of our greatest dilemmas – what is the best time or season to visit a country? I imagine we won't know until we've been everywhere!

After lunch, feeling more like having a siesta than a drive, Señor Jose and Marguerite drove us back to the airport with a very special experience on the way. We came through Papantla and some villages that looked like little versions of Gutierrez, only now in the post-siesta cool of the afternoon the people were outside in the streets. There was much more activity and quite a lot of traffic.

Marguerite told us we could not pass through Papantla without a visit to the ancient pyramid site of El Tajin. The Tajin took shape between AD 800 and 1150 and belongs to the Totonaca culture – the Indians who inhabited the east coast of Mexico and were the keepers of the secrets of vanilla until Montezuma blabbed to the Spanish. Tajin means 'The Sacred City of the Dead and of the Thunder in a Storm'. About six pyramids had been excavated and Señor Jose explained that the surrounding hills, which were covered with vegetation that looked particularly green in the yellow afternoon light, were also pyramids that had not been unearthed. These pyramids were much smaller than the ones we'd seen at Teotihuacan just outside Mexico City. They were far more intricate in their construction and instead of straight lines of masonry, they were gently curved – it seemed as though they were sagging – which was far more in keeping with their age. The pyramid Liz and I were most taken with was the Pyramid of the Niches, a construction with 365 niches, which coincide with the number of days in the solar year. The site had been beautifully restored and was well maintained with paths and mown edges.

As we were walking down the path away from the pyramids, Marguerite asked us to turn around and stretch our arms out with our palms facing towards the pyramids. Immediately we felt the most amazing pulse of energy against our hands and running up our arms, a tingling sensation as if a powerful infrared lamp was only a few centimetres away, shining on us. Marguerite said that most people experience the same sensation. She was pleased that we were in awe and offered no further explanation than the fact that it makes us all realise just how much we don't know.

We told Señor Jose and Marguerite not to wait at the airport with us. It was seven o'clock by now and our plane wasn't due until 8.20, and they still had a three-hour drive ahead of them to get home. We parted with only a modicum of friendly pressure to place an order for Gaya vanilla beans. This we firmly intended to do and finally did when we opened Herbie's Spices a couple of years later. Our flight back into Mexico City in the small plane was dazzling – city lights spread out like Inca gold as far as the eye could see.

As we landed in Mexico City to travel on to Spain and London we reflected on how much we had learnt about vanilla. Within six years, vanilla would be filling many of our waking moments and causing many nights of lost sleep. No, we had not contracted the affliction known as 'vanillism', an allergic reaction suffered by workers who are overexposed to vanilla. Its symptoms are headaches and lassitude. What happened over the next six years was a culmination of events that have plagued spice traders from time immemorial, caused by none other than – nature. In the late 1990s a series of severe storms and cyclones hit Mexico, the vanilla-producing countries off the east coast of

Africa and those well into the Indian Ocean. These massive storms decimated the vanilla crops and world prices for vanilla escalated sharply. That was not the end of it though; the following year's crop was a disaster because the vines that had been damaged developed a fungal rot. Consequently, the output of vanilla declined even further. Within four years of opening our shop the price of vanilla had risen five fold, and as I am writing, the quotations for premium grade Mexican and Malagasy vanilla are ten times higher than the 1997 prices.

This led us to search widely for alternate sources of supply that may help us satisfy our customers a little more economically. For a couple of years we had been receiving samples and prices for vanilla from New Guinea, a country that is geographically and climatically well suited to vanilla production. A fellow who shall remain nameless would telephone me every few months until I decided to trial a few kilos of his vanilla beans. Beginner's luck, they were beautiful, moist and plump. Although the flavour was not as complex and true as Mexican or Madagascar beans they were an acceptable lower-cost alternative. Buoyed by this success I ordered another batch and sent a telegraphic transfer for A$4,000 for the consignment my contact had promised. Ten months later I am still looking for my vanilla, my money and, more importantly, my supplier, who is no doubt in the jungle somewhere and probably cannot believe his good fortune in working out such an effective sting.

You have to keep your sense of humour, though. Recently I received a visit from another New Guinea supplier. This guy had really done his homework and was on his way to cornering the vanilla market. There was no chance of putting one over him and he held fast to the price he wanted, which was painfully close to that of Mexican and Madagascar beans. We had just run out of stock completely and it would be some weeks before we could get shipments from our reliable suppliers, so we struck a deal. He turned up at the shop a couple of days later all cock-a-hoop with a couple of kilograms of vanilla beans, and I cast a keen gaze over the prize that would put us back in the market for a few weeks. Would you believe it? The vanilla beans were sporting the first bloom of a batch of mould. Some people have confused mould with the appearance of vanillin crystals on the surface of vanilla beans. These crystals sometimes form at the end of curing and are usually considered to be a sign of very good quality, but if you look closely you will notice that they have a slightly elongated shape, a bit like Epsom Salts.

My mind went back to Mexico and the sobering thought that the producers in that part of the world had been curing vanilla for centuries. Every nuance at every stage of the process would be understood, monitored and considered. I felt sorry for my potential supplier who was crestfallen by the realisation that his batch of vanilla may be worthless. One can understand why a trader would be tempted to wash a batch of mouldy beans and try to dry them out again, maybe even soak them in a little vanilla essence to restore some of their aroma. People come into our shop and tell me what a great deal they got on this or that spice in some exotic market. I genuinely hope they did get a good deal. More often than not, though, what I am shown only reinforces that old adage that you usually get what you pay for.

SPICE SABBATICAL

Holidays can be dangerous things for Liz and me. Freed from the daily routine, a few days relaxation is all we need for our minds to start hatching another project. Maybe it is something as innocuous as redecorating a room or the whole house. Other more serious afflictions have led to moving home or building a new one. Basically we like projects, and on a sunny May afternoon in the Whitsundays, after the exhilaration of snorkelling off the Great Barrier Reef, Liz and I hatched a plan that was to be the third most significant change in our lives – after marriage and having our three wonderful daughters.

We were living on the Central Coast of New South Wales. We had moved there in 1991 when I was headhunted to work for a large food company that was based nearby. Kate and Marnie, our two eldest daughters, had left home and were working in Sydney and Sophie, our youngest, would be going to Sydney University the following year. Liz and I began pondering what we would do with ourselves over the next twenty or more years. Coming up to fifty, I knew that my 'use-by date' in the corporate world would approach before too long. I couldn't see myself wasting space until retirement and a golden parachute when I still had twenty years of work left in me. Liz was working part-time from home running the secretariat for the Food Media Club, but with the kids heading off to make their own lives, she could see she would soon have time on her hands.

Our discussion over afternoon coffee became more animated as we bemoaned the difficulty Liz was having finding spices for cooking. All the mainstream ones were readily available, I made sure of that in my marketing manager's role, but as for asafoetida (*Ferula asafoetida*), sumac (*Rhus coriaria*), or vanilla beans (*Vanilla planifolia*), they were hard to track down. We imagined a shop where you could buy every culinary herb and spice in one location, rather than having to hunt through half a dozen different ethnic grocery stores. We envisaged a place where only the very best quality spices would be sold. And most importantly we imagined a place where people could get advice. Advice on what makes one spice different from another and how it should be used and stored. We could see a need to demystify the magical world of herbs and spices and make them more accessible.

The logistics involved in starting a new business from scratch could be the subject of a book in its own right, and I won't impose that upon you now. Keeping in mind our penchant for travel to exotic climes, one of our first steps on the road to opening Herbie's Spices in July 1997 was to take ourselves on a 'refresher course' in spices – a spice sabbatical to the south of India, the ancient heart and present-day soul of the spice trade.

I had kept in contact with Mr Thampi, the publicity officer at the Indian Spices Board, since our first meeting at the International Spice Group meeting in New Delhi in 1986. Thampi had invited me to speak at the Spice Congress in Goa in 1995 and I decided to ask his advice on the best way to spend a month in Cochin, to learn as much as possible about the spice trade. He suggested we rent an apartment in the Ernakulam district, which he later arranged through a friend, and he would organise a program of visits to farms, processors and traders.

It was a time of hiatus. We had purchased a property in Rozelle, which happened to be the first one we looked at and its number in Darling Street was 745 – the same as my parents' herb nursery at Dural, which was 745 Old Northern Road. Spooky! We were waiting for council approval and I was still working at my corporate job. When my workmates heard that I was taking four weeks annual leave to have a holiday looking at spices, they thought old Herbie had really lost his marbles by taking a busman's holiday.

We left Sydney on New Year's Day 1997 and arrived in Mumbai at 10.30 pm on Liz's birthday, one she will never forget. We took a taxi from the airport to the moderately priced hotel we had booked from Sydney. This would have to be the worst hotel we had ever stayed in anywhere. Upon arrival we presented the confirmation of our booking and immediately knew we were not going to have an easy time. The misty-minded staff could not find any record of our reservation among the scraps of carbon-copy papers littered around the reception counter, impaled on office spikes and poking out of filing drawers. We seriously considered moving on to a Holiday Inn or some other more salubrious establishment, but thought for one night it couldn't be too bad. How wrong we were.

We were shown to an appalling room that we felt at the time was distinctly untidier, dingier and more spartan than the hessian structures Bombay's street dwellers resided in, and demanded something better. We waited in the foyer while a 'luxury suite' was prepared for us (perhaps they were building it judging from how long it took).

The hotel was like something out of a movie about the end of the world, when all order and maintenance had ceased for twenty years. Positioned in a beautiful location overlooking the sweeping expanse of Chowpatty Beach, it must have been quite grand when it was built. High ceilings, long corridors and a once ornate Victorian dining room may have accommodated Bombay's elite. Now, after about a quarter of a century of neglect, it was falling apart. You could see where door pulls and handles had been removed and replaced with cheap pressed-metal ones. In fact, any fitting or fixture of value had been stripped out long ago. The wall panelling was buckled and there were holes in the passageway ceilings, with sections of sheeting hanging down, apparently held in place by tenacious spider webs.

The 'luxury suite' was weird to say the least. The bathroom was made of the most beautiful, highly polished red granite – installed appallingly. The toilet plumbing didn't work and the shower was a furtive, lukewarm trickle, its water taking half an hour to creep sullenly away down the plughole. To add to the whole 'Twilight Zone' feel of the place, on closer scrutiny it became obvious that our 'suite' was actually a room within a room, as the old ceiling, cornices and walls could be clearly seen through the cracks, gaps and air vents in the ceiling.

One could hardly say we woke early because neither of us recalls actually sleeping. Liz had not eaten anything the night before but was as ill as someone who has eaten a rotten oyster. I pictured us being trapped in our granite room, mausoleum-like, if the building collapsed. Even checking out, which we were very keen to do as quickly as possible, was a challenge. The cashier had no change and said I would have to get it from the owner.

'So where is the owner?' I said.

''E is not 'ere, sir.'

'Well find him, ring him up, get him here so I can speak to him,' I remonstrated.

''E cannot be contacted, sir,' was the vacant reply.

Finally we waited until some other guests (who we had noticed through an open doorway were sharing six or eight to a room) paid enough cash on the way out to provide the cashier with our change. At A$200 for one night's accommodation, that will be the last time I try to book a so-called 'economical' hotel in India.

As the Indian Airlines domestic flight climbed out of the fetid Mumbai atmosphere Liz's tummy settled, and we looked forward to arriving in Cochin, or Kochi as the locals call it. Cochin is the capital of the state of Kerala on the south-western tip of India and is an ancient spice trading port surrounded by waterways. There are three main areas that constitute Cochin. The first is Ernakulam, which is the business centre with an enormous market area and many residences. Due west of coastal Ernakulam is a peninsula on which can be found the districts of Fort Kochi and Mattancherry. In between Ernakulam and Mattancherry is Willingdon Island, home to the luxurious Malabar and Casino hotels.

Our apartment in Ernakulam was spacious. It had three bedrooms, all with ensuites, and a basic kitchen and living area with French doors that opened out onto north- and east-facing balconies. Being on the fifth floor, there was nearly always a light afternoon breeze in the apartment that eased the tropical heat. Unbeknown to us, our landlord, Dr Anthony, who lived in a house next to the apartment block, had included our morning and evening meals as part of the deal. Liz and I would wait every day like chicks in a nest for Dr Anthony's cook, Stegie, to appear with the next culinary delight from the family kitchen.

On our first afternoon we ventured out into the streets and had a good old explore. Cochin is a relatively small city by Indian standards, with a population of about 1.7 million. Our five-storey apartment block, grand as it was, was situated at the end of a little dirt road surrounded by some very respectable houses and a few humble structures that would have looked more at home in the jungle. We walked past food vendors and soft-drink sellers, refraining from buying anything until we felt confident that our tummies had acclimatised. Crossing the first major road was a challenge. Traffic of all shapes and sizes was careering in all directions — lumbering, overladen, exhaust-smoke-belching trucks, three-wheeled yellow and black auto-rickshaws, Ambassador cars, little donkey carts pulling enormous loads, wobbly black bicycles and thousands of pedestrians. We hadn't seen any accidents so we figured there must be a secret, and we watched how the locals crossed the road. I must say they achieved a crossing with the greatest of ease, by gracefully and purposefully meandering through the melee.

After observing a few successful crossings we decided to shadow a competent-looking local. He spotted our intentions and gave us the Indian head-wobble of acknowledgement, fluttered his hand at the ground to indicate 'take it gently', and then walked out into the maelstrom. The secret is to walk slowly enough (saunter is a better word) so the traffic has time to see you and slow down marginally or swerve to miss you. To hesitate, speed up or demonstrate any lack of resolve in reaching your destination will lead to disaster. After a week we were enjoying playing in the traffic and looked back smugly over our shoulders at tourists cowering on the footpath, too nervous to venture forth. We did take pity on a few though, especially the enormous tough-looking German and his girlfriend who were mesmerised with fright on the kerb like a pair of rabbits stunned by a car's headlights.

Despite the promise of Stegie cooking for us, we wanted to buy a few supplies so we could prepare some meals for ourselves. Elated from the road crossing we went into a small supermarket and looked for the basics. In South India, the home of tea, all we could find was 'tea dust', which we were told was the best for 'making of tea'. Perhaps the best leaf tea is exported or only available from more elite retail establishments. We picked over the shelves, and were surprised by the number of different masalas (spice mixes) in packets. Many Indian families grind and blend their own spices, but no doubt convenience and consumerism are just as much a part of everyday lives here as they are elsewhere.

The new day was heralded by an early rooster at three in the morning, followed by a chorus of howling dogs and a lone, distant train whistle. Closer to dawn, some church bells rang, a train steamily tooted its departure, horns became more frequent, hawkers called and children played. Like an orchestra, the sounds of the day gradually came in one by one until the usual hum of background noise was established. We breakfasted on dosa, prepared by Stegie under the watchful eyes of Jansi, Dr Anthony's wife. Dosa is a popular breakfast in the South. It is a bit like a light pancake made from gram dhal (lentil flour) and uncooked rice, which is soaked, drained and ground to a batter. When Jansi offered us some chutney we expected the thick, sweet, spiced chutney we are familiar with in Australia. Instead she made what I have also heard referred to as a *chatini* of freshly scraped coconut, ginger, small onions, green and red chilies, curry leaves (*Murraya koenigii*), dried chillies, fried brown mustard seeds and salt to taste. She crushed the ingredients to the consistency of a salsa and we ate the chutney with the light, crisp dosa. It was a tantalising combination of fresh, lightly spiced flavours; just the thing to set one up for an excursion in search of pepper.

Thampi sent a car and driver to collect us and bring us to his office at the Spices Board headquarters in Ernakulam. I believe there are few people in the world as full of enthusiasm and joy as Thampi. Alternating between two telephones and sending stacks of papers flying, he indicated for us to sit in his office among piles of books, magazines, folders, papers and spice samples. The local language, Malayalam, is fired off from the voice box with machine-gun rapidity, which enhances one of the wonderful contradictions of Indian life. In an environment where everything sounds as if it is happening at a million miles an hour, getting anything done can be exceedingly slow. When speaking English, Thampi remains in rapid-fire mode, rolls his 'r's like an elocution teacher, gesticulates as if he has as many arms as Shiva, and has the warmth and expression in his eyes of a true believer. Arrangements had been made for Veeresh, a Spices Board field officer, to take us to see a 'spice garden', as many of the plantations are called. This is because a lot of the farms grow nutmeg, clove and allspice trees and have garden beds of turmeric and ginger along with the main crop of pepper.

We drove for a couple of hours north, then north-east, and stopped at the Spices Board's regional office at Malayattur. The local boss, a hyperactive, Indian version of Arthur Lowe (from *Dad's Army*), made a flurry of phone calls and said he would come with us to a pepper plantation. We back-tracked for almost an hour, then drove down a side road to a farmhouse which looked like a middle-class Singapore home. This was the home of his uncle, but we found out that Uncle's crop had been affected by disease that year and there was no pepper to see. We were beginning to learn the first lesson on being specific in India. We said we wanted to see a pepper farm. Fine, but did we say we wanted to see pepper being harvested or even pepper vines? No we didn't. So here we were at a pepper farm with no pepper!

More phone calls were made from Uncle's farm, while we sat on the verandah with Veeresh waiting for the outcome. We suspected success as we piled into the Ambassador and bumped over ever-worsening and narrowing roads accompanied by our four companions all talking at once.

In a scene that unfolded like a cinematographic

landscape, we emerged from the tree-lined road into a piece of paradise owned by a Mr George Peter. The road ended and we made our way on foot, trekking along narrow earth walls through a bright green rice paddy flanked by rubber and pepper plantations. We headed towards the pepper vines and clambered up the narrow steps cut into the loamy embankment. Our efforts were rewarded, as these vines were laden with spikes of plump green peppercorns. A picker, using a bamboo pole as a ladder, was harvesting the potent catkins of unripe pepper berries and putting them into a bag hanging from his shoulder.

The orderly rows of pepper vines trellised on palm trees were a particularly attractive sight. The pepper vine (*Piper nigrum*) is not a parasite, so the living palm tree simply provides an accessible trellis and its canopy of foliage gives shade for the vine, and for the pickers during harvesting. Pepper vines have dark green oval leaves that are shiny on top and pale on the underside. The leaves tend to average about 18 centimetres long and 12 centimetres wide. Six months earlier these pepper vines would have had minute flowers on long catkins hanging amongst the foliage. Pollination of the hermaphrodite flowers, a genetic characteristic of the most commonly cultivated varieties, is assisted by rain, which increases the efficiency of pollen distribution as water flows down the flower cluster. The fruits, or peppercorns, form in densely packed spikes, 5 to 15 centimetres long and over 1 centimetre wide at the thickest part near the top, and taper down to 5 millimetres or less at the tip. Each spike may produce fifty or more peppercorns which, when fully formed, are deep green. The peppercorns then ripen and turn yellow, and become a bright reddish pink when completely ripe.

The picker was gathering unripe berries because it is the green peppercorns that are dried in the sun to make the black pepper we know so well. Over the next few weeks, whenever we passed through pepper-growing areas, we would see woven mats out by the roadside with peppercorns drying on them. Like many spices, peppercorns contain an enzyme in the pericarp (outer skin of the berry) that is activated during drying. It is this enzyme that creates the volatile oil piperine which gives black pepper its characteristic aroma and flavour. For many years green peppercorns could only be purchased in brine, packed in little tins or bottles. The brine (a saturated solution of salt and water) inhibits the enzyme reaction so the berries stay green. Green pepper lacks the black pepper flavour, has distinctly fresh, green notes and is about the same heat strength as black. The only drawback with preserving green pepper in this manner is the high salt residue that needs to be thoroughly rinsed off the peppercorns before using them. To overcome this, research conducted in India about twenty years ago found that plunging green peppercorns into boiling water for twenty minutes killed the piperine-producing enzyme, making it possible to then dry the berries so they would stay green. These are the dried green peppercorns you see in mixes of peppercorns.

Ripe pink peppercorns from these vines have a delicious fruitiness and a distinct bite. Sadly they can only be bought in brine because any other method of processing causes their delicate structure to fall apart. When you do see dried pink pepper it is not true pepper, but the berries from a tree native to South America (*Schinus terebinthifolius*), which is cultivated on the Indian Ocean island of Reunion. A close relative of this tree (*Schinus areira* syn. *S. molle*) is the so-called pepper tree that is seen growing in many parts of Australia. The berries of this tree should not be eaten. It is also native to South America and was introduced to Australia, where its predilection for dry, hot conditions made it flourish in school yards, parks and by streams in many country towns.

White peppercorns, popular in Malaysia and Indonesia, are produced by removing the enzyme-containing pericarp from the berries before they are dried. Alternatively, the outer husk may be rubbed off black peppercorns mechanically, in a process called decortication. Because decorticated white pepper is difficult to produce and does not yield a good final product, the traditional soaking and macerating method, developed in Indonesia, is still preferred. This involves picking ripe fruits that are turning to yellow and pink. These berries are then tightly packed into gunny (hessian) sacks and immersed in water, preferably a clean, flowing stream, for between one and two weeks depending upon the ripeness of the fruit. During this period, and aided by bacterial activity, the outer husk softens in a process referred to as 'retting', which loosens it from the hard core. After being removed from the water, the macerated peppercorns are trampled and washed until no pericarp remains. When dried in the sun, or in ovens, these peppercorns remain creamy white because there is no enzyme there to turn them black. Thorough drying is crucial at the final stage, because if they are not properly dry, mould will easily form and give the white peppercorns a musty 'old socks' smell.

Veeresh pointed out a nutmeg tree (*Myristica fragrens*), and it was here in this spice garden that I was first captivated by the magic of opening a nutmeg fruit. Although it was a little early in the season for the full crop, Veeresh was lucky enough to find one ripe, nectarine-sized fruit on the tree. Mr Peter cut the fruit open, and the flash of wet, shining, blood red mace inside was breathtaking! The photo I took, with the pale fruit and red mace contrasting brilliantly against Mr Peter's dark hand, remains one of my favourites. The *aril* of mace is the placenta that conveys nourishment from the fruit to the seed. It clings to the shell of the nutmeg like a hand with its fingers holding so tightly that they leave little indentations to show where they've been on the brittle, dark brown shell. The wonderful glistening-wet look soon dulls as oxidisation takes place in the open air. Within a day of being placed in the sunshine, the mace will dry to the dull red-orange that you find on good quality dried mace. When it's in this whole or roughly broken form it is referred to in most recipe books as 'blade mace'. Mace is used in savoury cooking and complements fish and shellfish, and like nutmeg is delicious with spinach and with red vegetables such as carrot and pumpkin. The nutmeg in its shell is then left in the sun to dry and after a few days the dark, brittle shell is broken off, exposing the pale nutmeg itself. A nutmeg cut in half will reveal veins of dark brown oil cells, making it one of the oiliest of spices.

When buying nutmegs, one needs to be aware of their quality as it can vary enormously. When whole nutmegs have been stored for too long, something that may happen when prices are low and farmers hang onto them until the market moves up again, they begin to dry out. This loss of volatile oil, combined with insect attacks that leave tiny drill holes in the nutmegs, reduces them to an inferior grade. These are then referred to in the trade as 'BWP' (meaning 'broken, wormy and punky'), and when ground they yield a light brown, dry powder with not much flavour. Whole BWPs are useless in a nutmeg grater as they will crumble and not grate off in even, moist, aromatic shavings as expected from a higher-grade nutmeg.

I was keen to taste the pale flesh that surrounds the nutmeg and was impressed by its sharp astringency and lip-pursing bitterness. The flesh is sometimes used in pickles, where it has a similar effect as green mango. In parts of Asia it is pickled in salt and sugar and eaten as a confection. We could see that any processing of the flesh would have to be done immediately, because within a matter of minutes of opening the fruit it was oxidising and turning brown, in the same way as an apple does after it's cut. This is probably why the flesh of nutmeg fruit has never been processed on a commercial scale.

We arrived back in Ernakulam at three o'clock in the afternoon and had a late lunch of *thali*. An oversimplified description of *thali* is that it is similar to a banana leaf curry, but the meal is served on a large, round, stainless-steel platter. The rice is piled in the middle, and the rasam, sambar, curries, curds and pickles are placed in neat little stainless-steel cups dotted around it on the platter. I truly believe that I could eat *thali* for lunch every day for the rest of my life and never tire of it.

By now I was getting the urge to put pen to paper, as among the myriad daydreams Liz and I had discussed about our new venture, I felt there was the need for a really informative book on spices. I had never forgotten the Dickensian exercise books I saw in Connaught Place in New Delhi in 1986 and had it in my mind to buy one to start scribbling in. There was a little stationery shop just around the corner from our apartment, so I went there and found exactly what I was looking for: a cloth-bound, foolscap book with blue-lined, pale green pages. Each page had its folio stamped in red at the top, and judging by the placement of the numbers, it must have been done by hand. Five hundred pages in all, 3 centimetres thick and heavier than a laptop computer, this book was the ideal journal for me to record my experiences in. I also bought a bottle of black Indian ink and a new fountain pen that cost me the princely sum of three Australian dollars.

By the end of our first week in Cochin we were starting to feel very much at home and the locals were getting used to seeing us and trying to answer our silly questions. We would tend to do most of our excursions in the morning, have a late lunch, and then I would write during the afternoon in one of the bedrooms that I'd set up as an office. Hearing the sounds and catching the aromas drifting up from the streets on the afternoon breeze and occasionally gazing out over the city towards the ocean, it was easy to imagine Vasco da Gama arriving here in 1498.

One of our favourite lunch spots was the South Star restaurant on Marine Drive, a short and sometimes hair-raising trip from our apartment by three-wheeler auto-rickshaw. Thampi was taking us to the Pepper Exchange at Mattancherry the next day, so we decided to use this free time to have a shopping trip to get some Kingfisher beer and Kerala-produced bathtub gin. Naturally we would have to lunch at the South Star. We had prawns masala and a tomato paneer with rice and naan, preceded by a couple of fresh lime sodas. A fresh lime squeezed into a glass of cold soda water with a pinch of salt is a popular and very refreshing drink to have in this tropical heat and humidity.

The next day Stegie arrived with breakfast. Whole,

peeled, cooked bananas with a channel scooped out of the middle and then stuffed with freshly grated coconut. They seemed very plain compared to so many other meals, and I never really found out why they weren't at least spiced with some cardamom, nutmeg or cinnamon. Thampi collected us by mid-morning and we drove over the bridge to Willingdon Island, then over the next bridge to Mattancherry and Fort Cochin. The Pepper Exchange is in Mattancherry, the district in Cochin that is also home to the historic synagogue with its amazing display of blue, hand-painted Chinese tiles, so atmospherically described by Salman Rushdie in his book *The Moor's Last Sigh*:

> *No two are identical.* The tiles from Canton, 12″ x 12″ approx., imported by Ezekiel Rabhi in the year 1100 CE, covered the floors, walls and ceiling of the little synagogue. Legends had begun to stick to them. Some said that if you explored for long enough, you'd find your own story in one of the blue-and-white squares, because the pictures on the tiles could change, were changing, generation by generation, to tell the story of the Cochin Jews. Still others were convinced that the tiles were prophecies, the keys to whose meanings had been lost in the passing years.

Entry to the Pepper Exchange, just around the corner from the synagogue, is by invitation only, which can generally be arranged by the Spices Board for those of us in the spice trade. The Cochin Pepper Exchange works like the stock market with speculators, hedgers, futures and all the usual Bourse jargon. The experience is made truly exciting by hearing the trading taking place in the traditional 'open outcry' system. In what sounds and looks like chaos, all the buyers and sellers are shouting their contracts and bids in Malayalam, with a fury equal to sword-brandishing warriors in full battle. Amid the hubbub, these soldiers of fortune in their own private spice war manage to keep in contact with their clients from New York, Rotterdam, London and Singapore with a phone receiver in one hand while the other arm gesticulates furiously in punctuation of their cries. When we came back in 1999 computers had been installed and I thought the melee of traders would have become a thing of the past. I am happy to report that in spite of modern technology speeding up this process, the bombastic, charismatic pepper traders of Cochin still shatter the peaceful, tropical Mattancherry afternoon air with their excited 'open outcry' bids and contracts for thousands of tonnes of pepper.

That same day we met with Mr Ramkumar Menon (Ram), the manager of TATA Spices and the TATA pepper processing plant on Willingdon Island. Ram explained how their operations mostly involve tea, coffee and pepper. They own a number of plantations in the cool, tropical hills to the east that are known as the Western Ghats (*ghats* meaning steps, a range of hills or the roads going up hills), and so have a good grip on quality control. Over freshly brewed South Indian tea we discussed a number of 'spice issues' before looking over the pepper-cleaning operation. I was impressed by the attention to detail and quality standards here. The factory had a highly polished marble floor that would have been the envy of any grand hotel lobby. The ceilings were high, and the whole area was well lit by natural light. The range of pepper-grading and cleaning equipment was impressive and made it possible for TATA Spices to supply high quality pepper to world markets.

We had a day to fill in after our meeting with Ram and before seeing a contact Thampi had lined up for us. Some exploring around Ernakulam, followed by lunch, sounded like a good idea. For some strange reason I became absolutely convinced that I would be able to find a small mechanical spice grinder in the Ernakulam markets. Surely in addition to pestles and mortars, stone mills that weigh over 50 kilograms and are driven by an electric motor that could run a small sawmill, there must be something in between. We asked in one cookware shop and they sent us to the upstairs section of a shop across the road. Our queries then led us to the back where the shop was so crammed with ironmongery, pots and pans, cleavers and other cooking utensils that we thought they must have a spice grinder. As each bemused employee tried to help us we were processed through the shop and finally right out the back door! We were taken along a narrow walkway that was suspended like a fire escape above the lane, and in another door to the desk of the boss of the shop. Here we were seated while three pretty young girls tried to find what we wanted amongst myriad floor-to-ceiling stock. They kept bringing the wrong things until finally I drew a diagram of a grinder. 'Oh – a domestic grinder' the brighter of the three teenagers exclaimed and went to fetch exactly what we had been looking for. It was a miniature version of the plate mills I had seen grinding chillies in Singapore a decade ago, and I could not have been more delighted. The only drawback was that it was made of cast iron and weighed about 10 kilograms, so there wouldn't be more than one coming home in the luggage if Liz had any say in the matter (and she generally does).

Inspired by our success at finding the spice grinder we

celebrated with another lunch at the South Star, trying the specialty of the house, biriyani rice with chicken. The waiter told us they are famous for their biriyani and use 70 kilograms of rice a day. We were not disappointed with this fairly simple dish of lightly spiced chicken pieces served on yellow rice and spiced with cinnamon, cardamom, cloves, star anise, black pepper and chilli.

The following day we were fortunate to meet a young man by the name of Krish Menon. Thampi introduced Krish to us because he was working for a joint venture company in Cochin, AVT-McCormick, that had a modern, state-of-the-art spice-processing factory. Krish suggested we see some of the traditional spice processors before visiting their factory, no doubt to reinforce the stark contrast between their methods. Krish was joined by a large, imposing man called Sidi, a former pepper trader and now a buyer for AVT-McCormick. We soon realised that he had a wealth of knowledge about the spice trade in Cochin. After a cup of tea, lightly spiced with cardamom and cloves, we set off to Mattancherry and visited a pepper dealer's yard that was surrounded by a 2 metre high brick wall.

The significance of this excursion was not lost on me, as spread out in two-thirds of the 200 square metre area was mouldy black pepper. The other third of the yard was covered with glossy black peppercorns. The explanation – reconditioning, a practice that is much frowned upon within the industry. Reconditioning black pepper is a process whereby mouldy black peppercorns are sprayed with oil to make them dark and shiny, disguising the pale bloom of mould. Mould forms on pepper when it has not been properly dried, a once common practice when greedy farmers knew that a sack of pepper with 14 per cent moisture content would be heavier than a sack with 10 per cent moisture. So for a trader who has purchased pepper that is not dry enough and is developing mould, one solution is to recondition it. To the unknowing this scene was quite picturesque. Women in bright saris were raking furrows of pepper in the tropical sun and barefoot men were working ankle deep in shiny black peppercorns, as one batch after another was rhythmically sieved and bagged.

Our next treat was to visit a family spice-grinding and blending business run by a kindly old couple and their six sons. This time there was no evidence of underhand practices, just an insight into a very basic traditional factory. Piled in the middle of the floor was a mound of brightly coloured and multi-textured spices about a metre high. To this a young woman was adding curry leaves, stripping them straight from the branch and flinging them over the heap like confetti. When she had finished this, two men with shovels worked their way around the pile, turning and mixing the spices like a pair of labourers making cement. A primitive way to mix sambar spices, but certainly effective. The other basic yet effective process we noticed was the way some women filling cellophane bags with sambar powder were sealing the packaging material with a candle flame. When the bag is held in just the right position over the flame and then dexterously passed over it, the heat seal is made. We later saw a man doing this with a tube of different souvenir spices in one of the tourist shops in Mattancherry.

Krish collected us the next morning and took us to see the AVT-McCormick plant, which was about an hour's drive from Kochi, as we were starting to call our newfound home. The visit was preceded by tea and pleasantries with some of the management, who were attentive and interested to hear about the increasing market for spices in Australia. Liz and I donned white coats and hairnets, and were taken up five flights of stairs to the top floor where all the spices commence their processing journey, starting off as whole spices and finishing as ground spices packed in 25 kilogram bags. Using gravity to transport the spices, each of the five floors is used for different stages of processing. At the top the spice is graded and initially cleaned before proceeding through the following stages until the final ground product comes out at the end. Our guides were very proud of their steam sterilising section, which gives them the ability to produce spices with very low levels of bacteria, while avoiding the need to fumigate or irradiate them.

Our excursion wound up with the obligatory laboratory tour. After all, when you think of the huge investment in a well-fitted-out lab, it is no wonder everyone who has one wants to show it off. Krish dropped us back in Kochi in the afternoon and said he would meet us the next day to take us on a real journey back in time, to see ginger being processed in the way that it has been done for centuries.

We were starting to feel the aura of spices entering our bloodstreams. Whether riding up Mahatma Gandhi Road in an auto-rickshaw, or taking thali at the South Star, images of our shop and the way we would process our spices were beginning to form in our minds. How would we balance the traditional methods of spice grinding and blending with modern technology and Australian hygiene standards? At the time I underestimated the significance of this month in India. Unfettered by day-to-day issues we were able to daydream. We talked about the stainless-steel mixing machine we would need to buy, the mills we would require for grinding, and the tiled walls and stainless-steel benches to be installed in our packing room. It all contributed to our vision and reinforced the fact that no matter how clean and precise our business was to be, the impact of evocative aromas, eye-pleasing colours, a variety of textures and heavenly flavours could not be compromised.

A JOURNEY into the PAST

Krish arrived mid-morning to take us further out into the countryside. With images of mouldy peppercorns being reconditioned still firmly in our minds from the previous day, we wondered what example of ancient spice methodology we would see next. As it was late morning by now, we decided to have lunch at one of our favourite haunts, the Taj Malabar Hotel on Willingdon Island. We often stay at the Taj Malabar when we bring our Spice Discovery Tours to the south of India, because not only is it a beautiful hotel with exemplary service, but it is situated in one of the most picturesque parts of Kochi. It looks across the water to the peninsula of Fort Kochi, almost adjacent to the Dutch Palace and synagogue in Mattancherry. Dolphins are often seen lazily arching in groups of three or more in the fish-filled, protected waters. From this vantage point the Chinese fishing nets that dot the coastline up to St

Francis Church on the north-west tip of Fort Kochi can be seen silhouetted against the Lakshadweep Sea (the name given to this section of the vast Arabian Sea). Cochin was actually named by the early Chinese traders who came from Cochin China (present-day Vietnam), and introduced this ingenious method of fishing that has remained unchanged for centuries.

The Chinese fishing nets are large, spindly structures made from driftwood-grey poles lashed together with coir ropes. The manufacturing of coir fibre, from the abundant coconuts of south India, is a major industry, and the majority of coir mats sold around the world are made in Kerala. A large fishing net, about a third of the size of a bowling green, is lashed to spider-like poles rearing 6 metres into the air and hanging out over the sea. At the land end of the net, huge boulders act as counterbalances. Thus one or two men pulling on the ropes can lower the contraption into the water and raise it later when enough unsuspecting fish have swum into its clutches. There is nothing quite like a dusk water tour past these nets, when their ancient forms stand out against a reddening sunset, glowing on an inky sea.

Lunch at the Taj Malabar caters more to Western tourists than the local fare we had been eating, however it was a real treat to dine on rich korma curry and butter chicken along with seafood grilled with a simple spice of garam masala and chilli. The range of pickles accompanying the meals here is one of the most complete I have ever been offered. From familiar fennel, turmeric and green mango pickles to date and tamarind chutneys and one of my favourites, pickled spikes of green peppercorns that release a burst of salty, peppery flavour with each bite.

We were joined at lunch by one of Krish's associates, Sunil, and Mr George, a pepper and spice trader from the Kothamangalam area, as he was to show us the traditional manner of drying and cleaning ginger. Predictably we were in for a rough, two-hour drive in the same direction as Uncle's farm. Our first stop was at Mr George's agency in a small village whose narrow streets were crammed with heavily laden auto-rickshaws, ox-carts, donkey traps and lumbering, bald-tyred, suspension-challenged trucks. Mr George's godown was slightly wider than a terrace house and not much deeper. Dark, cool and windowless, the interior had a mystical atmosphere that became more familiar as one's eyes adjusted to the dim light. Then we were able to see that the room was stacked with ginger and pepper. The significance of just how many small farms are involved in the spice trade network was made patently obvious when a couple of men came in with a hessian shopping bag with about 10 kilograms of dried black pepper to sell. Mr George looked at it, placed it on the rusty beam-balance scales and after some haggling gave them 1000 rupees (about A$40).

Back in the car, we turned off the road onto a narrow, stony track. As the differential of the Ambassador banged on the centre mound and the wheels dropped into potholes, we prayed we would reach our destination before anything broke. Just as we were really beginning to wonder if we would ever get there, the car bounced, lurched and its overheated radiator wheezed as we emerged from the lush Keralan vegetation to arrive at a timeless scene covering about 5 hectares of rocky hillside.

Hundreds of farmers, who had leased small sections of the smooth rock face, were spreading their harvest of ginger

(*Zingiber officinale*) out to dry under the burning sun. Among this sea of ginger, small family groups were gathered in twos and threes under makeshift shelters of cloth draped over sticks. Their job was to roughly scrape the skin off both sides of the ginger root to speed up drying. This they did with the assistance of a steel sickle held between their feet, using both hands to hold the ginger.

Ginger root, or rhizome, is the knobbly part that grows and multiplies underground in tuberous joints. These are referred to in the spice trade as 'races' or more often and appropriately 'hands', because of their knuckled, arthritic shape that resembles the shape of a human hand. The smaller branches of the rhizome are logically enough called 'fingers'. Ginger rhizomes are encircled by scales, which form a rough, beige-coloured skin that covers the pale, creamy to white fibrous flesh. The aroma and flavour of ginger may vary considerably depending upon its variety, the stage at which it is harvested, and the region where it is growing.

Ginger rhizomes like the ones we saw here would generally be described as having a sweet, pungent aroma and lemony freshness. The flavour is similarly tangy, sweet, spicy and warm to hot, depending upon when it has been harvested. Ginger harvested early is generally sweet and tender, while later harvested rhizomes are more fibrous and pungent. Although ginger powder lacks the fresh, volatile aroma of the living rhizomes, it retains a spicy fragrance and characteristic ginger taste.

A combination of nearby cooking smells, tropical vegetation, sun-baked rock and ginger permeated the air. With not a mechanical device in sight, the fundamental simplicity was really brought home when we saw a couple of young men cleaning the dried rhizomes. They were standing facing each other, holding both ends of a hessian sack that contained about 3 kilograms of dried ginger, and were vigorously flapping it up and down with alternate arm movements like someone flipping sand from a beach towel. After a few furious minutes of agitation, during which time the abrasion between the rhizomes within the sack partially cleaned them, the man holding the open end let it go. The contents fell out onto the ground, revealing a pile of relatively clean ginger surrounded by a pile of flaky, easily winnowed away waste.

We once saw a ginger- and turmeric-cleaning method that was even more interesting. Like beached sailors, two men were seated opposite each other in a 'boat' about the size of a small dinghy. They had hessian sacking wrapped around their feet and in between them was a pile of ginger. To clean the ginger they were pushing their feet wildly backwards and forwards against each other (the way young children do when they are facing each other in a bath). The result – ginger again cleaned by abrasion.

No one knows for certain where this ancient spice originated, and it is not known to be growing in a genuine wild state anywhere, although it is cultivated in many tropical climates around the world. There are references to its cultivation by the ancient Chinese and Hindus, suggesting that ginger may have originated somewhere between northern India and east Asia, and it is recorded as one of the oldest Oriental spices to have been traded into south-eastern Europe. There are many stories about ginger; one tale recounts how a baker, in around 2400 BC on the isle of Rhodes near Greece, made the first gingerbread.

The beneficial properties of ginger have been recognised for centuries and were mentioned by Confucius (551–479 BC) and the first-century Greek physician, Dioscorides, who wrote the *Materia Medica*. Arab traders brought ginger into Greece and Rome, characteristically keeping their sources of supply from India a secret, and in the second century AD, ginger was included in the list of imports to Alexandria from the Red Sea that were subject to Roman customs taxes. It is also mentioned in the Koran, indicating to those virtuous enough to reach Paradise that they will not be denied the pleasure of ginger-flavoured water.

Ginger was referred to in England in the eleventh century and by the fourteenth century it was noted as the next most common spice after pepper. As ginger could be readily transported, growing in pots on board sailing ships without having to be processed, it was often the living rhizomes that were traded extensively during the Middle Ages. This led to ginger being transplanted to many countries, and just as the Arabs took ginger from India to east Africa in the thirteenth century, the Spanish established plantations in Jamaica in the sixteenth century. In Basel, the street where the Swiss spice traders conducted their business was called *Imbergasse*, which means 'Ginger Alley'.

We then noticed an area where the cleaned ginger was being put through a process that was definitely not ancient. In some countries bleached or white ginger is preferred. To achieve this we were shown where the ginger was piled up in mounds about a metre high. In the middle of each mound there was what looked like a wicker chimney rising up through the pile. With much ceremony, a few burnt fingers and a couple of false starts, a bowl of bright yellow, rotten-egg-smelling sulphur powder was lit and placed in the bottom of the chimney. Then the surrounding stack of ginger was covered with a tarpaulin to keep the sulphur fumes contained until they had their fumigatory effect and bleached the rhizomes to an insipid whitish grey. It is comforting to know that because consumers are now less likely to want a product treated with sulphur for simply cosmetic purposes, practices like this are gradually dying out.

For a spice that often tends to be taken for granted, the grading and marketing of ginger is somewhat complicated. In the spice trade, dry ginger is sold in eight grades and these indicate how the ginger has been prepared before grinding. Peeled, scraped or uncoated ginger refers to whole rhizomes that have had the outer skin cleanly removed without damaging the underlying tissue. Ginger processed in this way will have the best flavour. Rough, scraped ginger (which we had seen on the rocky hillside) has only had the skin partially removed from the flat sides to accelerate drying. Unpeeled or coated rhizomes have been dried intact with the skin still on. Black ginger, a term which is a little misleading, is used to describe whole live hands of ginger that have been scalded for ten to fifteen minutes in boiling water before being scraped and dried. The scalding kills the rhizome, preventing the likelihood of it sprouting, and it makes scraping easier and tends to darken its colour. Bleached or limed ginger describes clean-peeled whole rhizomes that have been treated with sulphur or lime. Splits and slices are unpeeled rhizomes, which have been split lengthwise or sliced laterally to speed up drying. Ratoons are the second 'crop' of rhizomes from plants that have been left in the ground for over a year. They are smaller, darker in colour, more fibrous and generally hotter.

My first impression of an Old Delhi street, its haze of wood smoke and cooking smells filled the air and thus began my enchantment with India.

Left: *I conduct an impromptu spice class in the markets, on our way to Ahmedabad.*

Chillies drying by the roadside in Gujarat, a common sight in these parts before the wet season.

Up to their ankles in mustard seeds, three young men sieve mustard in Gujarat.

*Bags of eye-watering chillies overflow at a merchant's godown, in the 'chilli town'
of Unja in Gujarat.*

Vanilla orchid flowers have to be fertilised by hand and even then only about 50 per cent bear pods.

Right: Vanilla pods ready to pick. At this stage they are completely tasteless and odourless.

Chinese fishing nets at dusk, Fort Cochin's romantic trademark.

Above: 'Uncle's pepper picker using a bamboo pole as a ladder in his 'spice garden' outside Cochin.

Fully formed but unripe spikes of green peppercorns ready for picking.

Peppercorns drying on mats by the roadside, a familiar sight in Kerala between December and February.

A nutmeg fruit cut open to reveal the glistening aril of bright red mace that surrounds the nut.

*Blade mace, which turns light brown as it oxidises during drying,
on sale in the Ernakulam markets in Cochin.*

Very basic ginger drying and cleaning on our 'Journey into the Past'.

The Sediyapu family who were so hospitable to us. On the far right is our dear friend Dr Thampi, and beside him is Satir, head of the organic spice farmers' co-op near Mangalore.

Mrs Sediyapu removes the tamarind seeds from the pulp, collecting them in a practical, palm-frond tray.

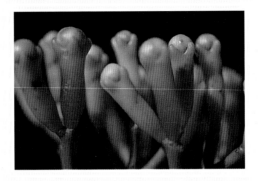

Clove buds just picked and ready to dry. During drying an enzyme reaction turns them dark brown and creates a volatile oil called eugenol.

Buyers lined up at the cardamom auction at Vandamettu.

Cardamom capsules form at the base of the plant when the racemes have finished flowering. They are picked when plump, but before they ripen and split.

A young elephant comes to the water's edge to play in the Periyar wildlife sanctuary at Thekkady.

Young women of marriageable age bringing their offerings of sprouts, an indication of prosperity for that woman's family for the next year, and of her potential fecundity.

One of the many spice merchant's stalls in the covered markets in Istanbul.

Plump, ripe sumac berries ready for processing.

Ageing, atmospheric alleys like this one crisscross Stone Town on the island of Zanzibar.

*Scarlet annatto pods,
which are full of tiny, deep
red seeds, dry and look like
Oscar the Grouch.*

Dzoanh demonstrates peeling cassia bark in whole pieces from an eight-year-old tree.

Below: *Cassia buds.*

Scraping dried cassia scrolls to inspect the oil line, an indication of volatile oil strength.

Cassia scrolls stored like manuscripts in an ancient library.

Kitty gathering bush tomato (akudjura) on Napperby Station in Central Australia.

Bush tomato flower.

Bush tomatoes that have dried on the bush and are ready to pick.

Kitty retrieves a plump witchetty grub from the roots of a witchetty bush.

Liz and me inside the shop.

One of my favourite photographs: Mr Peter cuts open a nutmeg to reveal the bright red mace.

The groups of workers toiling on the hillside were somewhat bemused, and I dare say entertained, by our serious deliberations on all aspects 'ginger' and our deep interest in their seemingly mundane daily chores. Right on cue, as if to reinforce Krish's comments on the need to modernise this outmoded form of processing, a truck backed up to an embankment to load on a cow and her calf. Gently belligerent and unwilling to comply with her handlers' intention to get her and her calf on the truck, the soft-eyed Jersey danced and sprayed nervous dung all over the ginger. No one noticed, and after mother and calf were safely onboard, the group near the ginger continued with their routine.

Our hosts, knowing that we wanted to see as much as possible while in this region, informed us of the existence of large turmeric plantations in the same area. Turmeric is related to ginger and the rhizomes look very similar when harvested. That is where the similarity ends, though, as turmeric contains a powerful colouring agent called curcumin and has a distinctly earthy aroma and flavour. Fresh turmeric is used in some Asian recipes, however the powder is the most common ingredient in Indian cooking. Turmeric's reputation has often been besmirched by dodgy traders selling it as 'saffron powder' or 'Indian saffron'.

We had travelled for hours over rough roads to find the ginger, but that was only the beginning when it came to looking for the turmeric. Mr George said the plantation was not far away, so off we headed down another narrow track, the wheels of the Ambassador again just straddling the hump in the middle of the road. We had to get out and walk a few times because the car was bottoming out on ground that would have been more regularly traversed by bullock cart. The sun began to set and we wondered if we would reach the plantation before dark. Finally arriving at an open area, the driver pointed out a mud-brick shed that housed harvested turmeric waiting to be cleaned and sent to market. As we surveyed the freshly dug field, lit by a full moon shining through a fine grey-pink haze, we asked where the turmeric plantation was. The reply – this was it; all the turmeric had just been harvested!

It was just as well we had such a wonderful experience seeing the ginger drying as I am sure not many people would have travelled as far and as long as we did that day to gaze upon a turmeric plantation with no turmeric growing. We have a timeless image in our minds of the undulating land-scape studded with coconut palms at the end of an almost inaccessible track some hours' drive outside Kochi. The stored, recently uprooted turmeric smelled of a sharp earthi-ness and was quite pungent. Whenever I smell good quality turmeric now, it takes me back to the same earthy smell of that turmeric storage shed.

The trip back was a little hairy because at night many drivers prefer to keep their headlights turned off unless absolutely necessary because they believe it saves their batteries. After a long hot day, we dozed in the back of the Ambassador as it weaved its way home. We thought we were familiar with the sounds and chaos of cars and bikes around us until we passed an area where lantern-lit tents lined the road and thousands of people milled around outside in the darkness. Suddenly there was a white flash of light and a thundering explosion rocked the car. Were we about to be attacked? 'Bloody hell!' I exclaimed, wondering what was going to happen next. The driver laughed;

it was just celebrations for St Simeon's day. As we drove on through more villages we saw similar celebrations with church processions along the road, fireworks, sideshows and huge crowds.

Many Christians live in Kerala, and there are constant reminders of this in the number of magnificent, Portuguese-style churches that one sees while driving through the jungle. We were taken with the way Indians, not surprisingly, celebrate their Christianity in such an Indian manner! Elephants bedecked in finery lead church processions; noise, smoke, food-smells and very loud fireworks are all part of their religion.

As our minds were turning more and more to our shop, we could not help thinking that every item of interest we saw was potential merchandise. We had to keep reminding ourselves that ours was going to be a spice shop and should not waver from that by stocking anything else. However, when Thampi mentioned an old friend of his called Jerson, who had a small woodworking business on Willingdon Island, we pictured the charming spice boxes, like the 'antique' ones sold to tourists in the Mattancherry district, and we were very tempted. I say 'antique' because the majority of these rustic finds in dusty, cobwebbed corners of countless curio shops are just manufac-tured from old timber.

Jerson's workshop was situated down a long, narrow road that was flanked by 2 metre high, once-white concrete walls, surrounding properties that averaged a hectare or two in size. We turned into his driveway and stopped in the shade of a grove of trees at the front of the house. It was like many others we had seen, built of concrete with thick walls and large doorway and window openings to let the air circulate. As is customary, we sat on the verandah and were offered tea and cool drinks while we discussed our spice-related merchandise with Jerson. He was keen for us to see his factory behind the house, where workers stood in piles of wood shavings at lathes and sanding machines, and a layer of fine ochre sawdust covered every surface like dirty snow. Machines whined, belt drives hummed and wobbled as exposed shafts spun wildly. I winced at the thought of how easily a finger could be ground, sliced, skinned or crushed, if it got in the way of any of these machines.

The inspection complete, Jerson sat us down once again as he retrieved his samples and explained the quality of his work. He showed us some beautifully made little smoking pipes that had been the cause of much recent misfortune. The workshop had made thousands of these pipes to be sent to America. When they were finished, the contract fell through because US Customs banned them on the basis that they could be used for smoking illegal substances. He kindly offered us some for free, but knowing Australian Customs to be equally suspicious, we declined the opportunity of taking a few home.

What did catch our eye, though, were little pestles and mortars made of rubberwood. The mortar was about 6 centimetres in diameter and hollowed out inside, with a small hole in the top less than 2 centimetres across. The pestle then fitted snugly into the narrow hole so that when the mortar was held upside down, the pestle would dangle and not fall out. You could fill the mortar with about two teaspoons of spice seeds and grind away furiously while talking. For this reason Thampi christened them 'talking pieces'. At first we thought they were a bit gimmicky but we discovered that a spoonful of mustard seeds could be crushed without them flying out all over the room.

We finished the meeting by giving Jerson an order for a couple of hundred talking pieces and told him we would give him a 50 per cent deposit and pay the balance when they arrived in Australia. Although they were a bit of fun, they turned out to be one of the slowest-selling items we carried, so sadly we did not re-order.

ORGANIC SPICE GARDENS in MANGALORE

Three weeks had passed in our beloved Kochi and although we were looking forward to going home and seeing our girls again, we also felt that we could quite comfortably spend six months here. Our trip to the cardamom hills and beyond to Thekkadi was scheduled for the following week; before then our plan was to travel by train to Mangalore and visit a group of organic spice farmers in the area. Our bags were packed and ready but in classic Indian fashion we still did not know if we could get a ticket on the overnight train. Thampi finally phoned to say the train tickets were confirmed. The 400 kilometre journey north, up the west coast of Kerala to where it meets Karnataka state and the coastal city of Mangalore, would take all night so he had booked berths in a sleeper car for us.

Before catching the train we dashed up Mahatma

Gandhi Road to change a traveller's cheque, and on our way back slipped into the Avenue Regent Hotel and enjoyed a Kingfisher beer in the air-conditioned bar. The coolness permeated right through the layers of our tropically heated bodies. The Avenue Regent had become a regular haunt and I'm sure the staff thought we were guests there, having seen us so often. It was our own little scam when the apartment, despite the breeze, was getting altogether too hot and we needed some cool respite. We would walk into the lobby looking completely at home, sit in the comfortable lounge chairs and read our books or discuss our next move. Then after a cooling ale in the bar, we would walk out the back entrance where the hotel taxis were waiting and tip the concierge who helped us into the next Ambassador to pull up and whisk us away. The destination might be Fort Kochi or Willingdon Island for more Walter Mitty daydreaming about just staying here and trading in spices like a sixteenth-century merchant.

After dinner, Thampi met up with us and we walked a kilometre to the railway station and caught the Malabar Express, which left on time. A guard in Indian Railways whites, beautifully pressed if somewhat soiled, came around and issued every passenger with two sheets, a grey blanket with the ubiquitous blue stripe down the middle and a tiny pillow. Each compartment had four bunks, double-decker style, facing each other, with a curtained sleeping alcove made of two folded-down seats running lengthwise on the other side of the corridor. We slept surprisingly well. The only downside to travelling at night was not seeing towns such as Chaavakkaad, Kozhikode and Pondicherry on the way. We arrived at Mangalore at 9.30 am and were greeted by the head of Magosan

Exports, the organic growers' co-operative. For our tongues he had a long, unpronounceable name but Thampi reeled it off, gatling-gun-style, and suggested we call him Satir. Satir was a slight, wiry, almost hyperactive man with intense dark eyes and a passionate opinion about everything. His Tata station wagon, which looked like a Landcruiser but was not four-wheel drive, had the necessary ground clearance for these roads and a bone-shattering suspension to match its utilitarian appearance. Before heading out of town we breakfasted on potato masala dosa, a pancake made with wheat flour and folded around cooked, spiced potato. After breakfast we made a brief stop at the hospital, where Satir's neighbour was in a state of shock after a truck had run over his motorbike, killing his pillion passenger. It was a sober reminder that although the 'shoal effect' of traffic movement here seems to work effectively, it is just as fallible as any other traffic system. The man had lain by the roadside all night, until someone in the morning realised he was injured, not drunk.

Mangalore had most of the bustling, contradictory elements you will find in many Indian cities, a notable exception being the undulating topography and haphazard street layout. Visitors could easily get lost here so we appreciated the guidance of our local host. Satir's farm was two-and-a-half to three hours' drive from town; on the way we would drop into an organic farm that produced pepper, cloves and allspice. We took the main Mangalore to Mysore road, which deteriorated soon after leaving the outskirts of Mangalore into a succession of ruts, cracked tar and potholes. After a couple of hours of lurches and bumps, our clothing sodden from perspiration, we were a little relieved when Satir turned off the main road into state forest. It was quite beautiful and more lush than the dusty countryside we had been passing through.

The road eventually led to a narrow dirt track, which ended at the farm of Mr Butt, an ex-school headmaster turned organic nurseryman and farmer. His stone home was idyllically placed in this remote and peaceful location. Satir's enthusiasm was balanced by Mr Butt's authoritarian demeanour, an aura no doubt developed over years of teaching. Mr Butt was used to having an attentive audience that hung on his every word and I can truthfully say we were no exception. He showed us his nursery where he was propagating pepper vines, vanilla orchids, clove, nutmeg and allspice trees. The notion of the Indians producing vanilla seemed a logical one, given the climatic conditions and the familiarity they have with labour-intensive processing. Although we had learnt more about vanilla on our last trip to Mexico than Mr Butt could probably tell us, we were highly impressed with his passion and willingness to share his knowledge.

The farm tour commenced with a walk through a grove of coconut palms that were supporting pepper vines. A wide creek interrupted our stroll to the undulating slopes that were planted out with clove, nutmeg and allspice trees, however there was a round pole bridge from one bank to the other. Liz allowed discretion to be the better part of valour, but not wanting to miss anything I took off my shoes, hoping to achieve some semblance of a monkey-like grip on the slippery pole, and ventured forth. Mr Butt and Satir scampered across with agility while Thampi waited with Liz. I also decided to take the log at pace, hoping my momentum would take me to the other side before gravity won the day. Obviously the Spice God was watching over me, because in an uncharacteristic demonstration of athleticism and composure, I scurried over the log with the alacrity of a water rat.

It was worth taking the chance, as here I was surrounded by a majestic stand of allspice trees. The bark of allspice trees is aromatic and silvery grey, and contains a hard, durable, close-grained wood, which was used for making walking sticks in the nineteenth century. This practice was stopped by legislation in their native Jamaica for fear of the destruction of the economically valuable trees. Smelling the leaves grouped in clusters at the end of the slender branches reminded me of Bay Rum aftershave and the name Bay Rum Berry Tree that is often given to allspice.

Back at the house, having successfully navigated the dreaded log again, we sat in comfortable wicker chairs on the wide, cool verandah where Mrs Butt had set out dishes of homemade snacks. As we tucked into little pakoras, nuts roasted with spices and savoury banana chips, Mr Butt chopped the ends off fresh coconuts and poured refreshing coconut water for us all. The concept of warm country hospitality seems to be the same, whether in India or Australia, and we noticed it at every farm we went to. Sitting around drinking water or cordial (never alcohol) is an integral part of these visits, and we have learned to be patient and go with the flow. It hadn't taken us long to realise that a fleeting visit to look at a few spices and then buzzing off again was close to impossible, but the extra time taken made it far more enjoyable.

Farmers are similar all over the world, and Mr Butt and other farmers we met often couldn't help themselves from giving Thampi a lecture on how much more the Spices Board could do for them, by way of subsidies and other assistance. Thampi, to his credit, always fielded these comments with innumerable examples of what the Spices Board does accomplish for growers, and assured them that their suggestions would not go unnoticed.

With at least another hour's driving to reach Satir's farm, we took our leave, having enjoyed our time with these charming and hospitable people. We arrived in the early afternoon at another tropical paradise, surrounded by tall, shady trees. The warm, loamy smell of damp, fertile earth and wood smoke filled the air. Satir stopped alongside a recently built, concrete-block cowshed of which he was very proud. We couldn't see a house and wondered just where we would be staying – a cowshed may have been appropriate for a homeless couple about to give birth two thousand years ago, but that was not quite the experience we had in mind. As we rounded the cowshed, however, we saw the old homestead squatting as it had for two hundred years – seven generations of Satir's family had lived here.

It was surrounded with the pinky-red clay we had seen in many parts of Kerala. Indians don't grow and tend manicured lawns the way we do. The yard here is covered every couple of weeks with a cowdung slurry that dries in the sun and makes a hard, easily swept surface that prevents dust from blowing around in the dry season. The baked slurry washes away during the monsoon and when the wet season has finished, the fortnightly ritual of re-surfacing the yard starts again. A square pot of holy basil (*Ocimum sanctum*) or *tulasi* as it is called in India, was positioned on the eastern side of the house near a doorway, as is the custom. The Indians believe it to be sacred and that it will protect the household. Holy basil has mauve-pink flowers, is a perennial and is lightly lemon-scented. Although its perennial habit has increased its popularity in Australian gardens, I really think the flavour is too pungent to be a substitute for sweet basil (*Ocimum basilicum*).

On the southern side was a garden of sweet-smelling roses, hydrangeas and other flowers. The embankment on the northern side went down to a well-trodden earthen track that was used by the villagers to get to the coconut and pepper gardens nearby. Further around, on the western side, there was a 500 year old well, with water that Satir swears is pure.

An area about half the size of a tennis court was covered in areca nuts (*Areca catechu*) drying in the sun. Areca nuts are sometimes incorrectly called betel nuts because they are chewed with betel leaves (*Piper betle*) for *pan*, a mouth-reddening, tooth-decaying, hypnotic concoction that is so popular among Indians. Areca nuts are covered with a fibrous shell the size of a small nectarine, and actually come from a variety of palm that looks like a small coconut palm. When the husk is removed, the areca nut (or the seed) looks just like a large nutmeg.

Beyond this drying area was more garden and another embankment with a dozen or so steps, leading up to a rustic building. 'Oh, no!' Liz muttered under her breath to me. 'Please don't let this be the guesthouse.' Luckily it wasn't; it was the packing shed for the spices, rudimentary yet effective. I loved the ginger- and turmeric-cleaning device. It was a barrel-sized cylinder about 2 metres long and a metre in diameter, constructed of unsawn branches with wire netting stretched over them and pivoted on an axle that ran from one end to the other with a 'crank handle' at one end. The cylinder is filled with dried ginger rhizomes, and when the handle is turned the agitation of the ginger inside the rough-hewn, wire-covered cylinder cleans its contents. Although somewhat primitive in appearance (it looks like the kind of thing Fred Flintstone would use) it was relatively modern when compared to the 'flapping sack' or 'foot-slapping boat' used by others.

We settled into the farmhouse and relaxed on the verandah until we were called for a late lunch at a quarter to five. Satir ushered us into a dim room, bare except for a table and chairs. With no electric light and the fading daylight filtering through the tall trees surrounding house, we felt incredibly peaceful. Silent dark forms flitted back and forth serving the food while the only conversation was between Satir, Thampi, Liz and myself. We ate a satisfying meal of rice and home-grown vegetable curries followed by banana halva.

After lunch we got down to discussing secret spice merchant's business and had our first impressions of Satir strongly confirmed. A man who is passionate about his beliefs, he has a healthy distrust of all politicians. He has a degree in education, a voluable grasp of English and a formidable knowledge of plants and their properties. His belief in nature is the basis of his philosophy of farming and living. While he has spent *lakhs* (hundreds of thousands) of rupees on his farm and getting international organic standards approvals for his produce, he sees no need to spend money on his home, as his needs for living are simple. He told us how he and the other growers in the co-operative got into organic farming. About twenty years ago a number of pepper shipments from India to the United States were rejected because their pesticide residues were too high. This really annoyed the Indian producers, because, yet again, it was the Americans who had been selling chemical pesticides to the Indian growers in the first place. To compound their problems, many farmers were finding that their vines were less healthy and their yields were lower than they were in their fathers' and grandfathers' days. A group of farmers decided to find out what earlier generations had done. After all, they had been farming right here on this very soil for a couple of centuries before chemicals came along. According to Satir, the fundamental basis of this earlier farming had been what we now acknowledge as organic farming. The co-op farmers have the advantage of modern technology – they use solar power to generate electricity, methane production from waste to power engines and have a general regime of 'no waste', making all their resources as productive as possible.

Their practice of multi-cropping seems to keep plant disease at bay, and Satir successfully uses companion planting and biodynamic farming methods. When I asked him what he would do with a diseased plant, he explained that rather than pull it out and try to eradicate the disease he will pulverise some of it and make it into a spray to put on all the others. Instead of spreading the disease this practice has a vaccinating effect on the healthy plants.

We were engrossed with what Satir was telling us, but a tide of weariness was beginning to rise. I think it was noticed, as our host offered us sarongs to wear and asked if we would like a bath. Satir's son led us by lamplight around the kitchen and along a narrow path from the house to the most wonderful washroom we've ever used. A fire in the outside wall heats a copper of water until it is almost boiling. The top of the copper is set in a concrete bench about waist height. Also on the bench is a big plastic bowl under a cold water tap, a copper ladle, a copper bowl and a couple of hollows in the bench for a cake of soap. Part of the bench slopes so it can be used as a washboard if you choose to wash your clothes with your left-over warm water. The floor was concrete, with a stone block about 30 centimetres high and wide dividing the floor in half. One half wet, one dry – so logical. Three ladles of hot water mixed with cold made a whole bowl of steaming bath water, and tipping it over oneself ladle by ladle was a basic, enjoyable experience. It was somehow sensual and leisurely, relaxing for the psyche as well as cleansing the body.

Once clean and comfortable in our sarongs, we sat around and, of course, discussed spices. Satir was very proud of his sample of what he called vanilla sugar. Now vanilla sugar as we know it is a mixture of caster sugar and artificial vanillin powder. Satir's product was the scrapings of pure vanilla crystals from vanilla beans he had cured. This got me very excited, because although I had seen small amounts of vanilla crystals on cured beans, I had never heard of anyone being patient enough to actually collect them. I think Satir found the process more demanding than he expected because after we opened the shop he was never able to supply this heavenly product in commercial quantities. I dare say, if it ever became available it would rival saffron in cost.

We had a light dinner at about ten o'clock, again just the four of us with the family hiding in the background, and Satir commented on the way we looked quite comfortable eating with our hands. Our friends in Singapore had shown us how easy it is to scoop the food up in your fingers and push it into your mouth with your thumb. Satir said he could not understand how Westerners can indiscriminately shovel food into their mouths with forks and spoons, without touching it first. How else would you know how hot it is, or feel its texture? Satir even claimed to be able to tell the degree of chilli heat in a meal from touch.

When we retired for the night, two biscuit-thin mattresses had been laid out on the hard floor. The wooden shutters were open and the glassless windows let in the cool night air. After our train journey the night before and the full day we'd had, we fell deeply and soundly asleep.

We heard sounds of activity at dawn, including the noise of the grinding stone, which was tended by a woman who seemed to be chopping, grinding, grating and preparing food all day long. Buckets clanked, cows walked softly and steadily towards the milking bales, and brief early-morning chatter drifted on the fresh air. By the time we emerged, Thampi and Satir were having an animated discussion about pepper standards and waiting to take us for a pre-breakfast walk. On a track leading down to the village we met workers on their way to the farm, and were impressed by the practicality of the hats they were wearing. They were made from the base end of a palm frond, pinched together at the front and back and worn as jauntily as an American GI cap.

Satir stopped to show us a vine of long pepper (*Piper longum*), which looked quite different from the pepper vines we were becoming so familiar with. Long pepper vines grow in India and Indonesia and they are slender climbers that have sparser foliage than standard pepper. The most noticeable difference between the two is that the fruits of Indian long pepper are smaller and less pungent than those of Javanese long pepper

(*Piper retrofractum*). It is called long pepper because the fruits are long cylindrical spikes about 5 millimetres in diameter and 2.5 to 4 centimetres long. Each rough, dark brown to black, spike resembles a male pine flower catkin, which when broken and looked at in cross section, reveals a cartwheel of up to eight minute, dark red seeds. Satir explained that long pepper is used for relieving coughs and colds, and when I tasted the tiny fresh fruit I noticed how refreshing and antiseptic-tasting it was. When dried, long pepper has an extremely sweet aroma, like a cross between incense and orris root powder. The taste is bitingly hot, lingering and numbing, belying its innocent smell.

After a simple but tasty breakfast of *iddli* (little steamed wheat and gram dhal cakes that are eaten with rasam, coconut chutney and pickles), we walked over to Satir's father's house about half a kilometre away. The walk was characteristically idyllic, along a well-worn track through dense foliage, past clearings planted out with ginger and turmeric (yes, we actually got to see a few acres of turmeric before it was harvested), and groves of cinnamon and nutmeg trees. Satir would point out every plant that could be put to some useful purpose. I could easily have spent a couple of days making notes of all the details he was telling us. To Satir, nature provides everything that is required for health, pleasure and happiness. He is very much in touch with reality as well, and far from living the simple life, he uses technology such as solar power, and a computer to access the internet.

Again we were greeted with warm rural hospitality, as Satir's mother brought out homemade snacks and kokam (*Garcinia Indica choisy*) water. Kokam is a fruit often used in the south of India as a tangy substitute for tamarind or lemon juice.

We asked about a huge iron pot, about 3 metres in diameter and 1.5 metres high, which was sitting in an open-sided barn. 'That is used for making parboiled rice or Kerala rice, it is very popular in the south of India. It is good for the digestion,' Thampi explained, rubbing his tummy and no doubt already thinking ahead to our next meal. The food is so absolutely wonderful here that it is difficult not to become preoccupied with it. We sat on the shady verandah talking to Satir's parents while nibbling spicy tidbits and washing them down with bright pink kokam water.

Back at Satir's farm we loaded our gear into the car, Mrs Satir gave us some home-made banana halva and salted banana chips to take with us, and we ventured forth again to visit another of the organic farmers in the area.

After passing hundreds of cashew trees coated in pinky-red dust, we came to the Sediyapu family farm. We passed through freshly painted gateposts and large wrought-iron gates to a well-swept parking area, a neat two-storey house, and a garden of myriad colourful flowers surrounded by well-trimmed hedges. Again there was no lawn, and as with Satir's house, there was a pot of holy basil at the entrance. Home to an extended family, it felt welcoming and comfortable as we sat on the verandah and refreshed ourselves with coconut water. Cricket was showing on the television, and we found it amusing that the family thought we would be experts on cricket because we are Australian. It is a sobering reminder that your ethnicity does not automatically make you an expert on a subject. After opening the shop we would have customers come to us and make some doubtful comments about a spice. When we questioned the authenticity of the information they would respond with, 'But it was an Indian (or Thai, Ceylonese, African, and so on) who told me, so it must be true.' If that is the case we could tell the Indians anything that came into our heads about cricket, and they would then say to their mates, 'But it was an Australian who told me, so it must be true.'

After initial pleasantries, we strolled to a building near the house where the little family business makes cordials, their specialty being kokam cordial (they call it *birinda*). The neat two-room building had one area with stainless-steel vats for boiling the syrup and another for filling the bottles and labelling them. This was the same kokam cordial we had tasted at the Satir Senior household, and we took the opportunity to look at a nearby kokam tree. It was slender and graceful, about 15 metres high with medium density foliage of oval, light green leaves. The fruit looks similar to a small plum and turns dark purple when it is ripe. The Sediyapus harvest them when they are ripe, and using only the rind, which comprises about 50 per cent of the whole fruit, preserve it by drying it in the sun. Sometimes salt is rubbed into the rind to speed up drying and assist with preserving the leathery morsels. To make the tangy, refreshing, deep purple cordial they boil the kokam with sugar syrup. Our hosts assured us that taken regularly the cordial would be beneficial in reducing obesity and cholesterol.

Kokam is also used in cooking in much the same way as tamarind. The dried, flattened rind is usually sold in small, leathery pieces about 3 centimetres long, which can be unfolded into a half-fruit-sized skullcap. The aroma is slightly fruity and faintly balsamic with notes of tannin. A closely related spice grown in Asia is assam gelugor (*Garcinia atroviridis*). It has similar acidic properties to kokam and the confusing name of tamarind slices, when dried and sliced, which they are not. Speaking of confusion, we have noticed that many cooks in the south of India call kokam 'fish tamarind', a name that reinforces its tamarind-like acidity and its appropriateness with seafood.

Lunch was eaten with Liz, me and the menfolk while Mrs Sediyapu and her smiling daughters looked on, making sure our plates were never wanting for another pile of steaming Kerala rice or a spoonful of dhal, curried vegetables, sambar or rasam. We were becoming very fond of the parboiled rice. It has little purple lines on one side of the grains and they have a consistency and flavour that goes hand in hand with the wonderful array of flavours in the food.

Our post-prandial stroll took us back past the kokam tree and down a long track, which was quite open and less tropical than the land around Satir's farm. We were on our way to see a grove of old tamarind trees (*Tamarindus indica*). Tamarind trees bear 10 centimetre long fruits that are knobbly, light brown pods containing an acidic pulp that surrounds about ten shiny, smooth, dark brown, angular seeds, measuring roughly 4 millimetres by 10 millimetres. The bulbous, knuckle-like pod has a brittle shell, which when broken away reveals a pale tan, sticky mass with longitudinal strings and fibrous veins attached.

When one stands beneath these grand tall trees, it is difficult to imagine how these long, curved pods could possibly be picked. We soon learnt, when one of the Sediyapu family pointed up into the higher branches and all of a sudden the upper foliage of a majestic tamarind tree began to quiver furiously. High up a man was shaking the branches to dislodge the fully developed pods, which were falling to the ground in a clattering hailstorm.

We then gathered up the pods and took them to the house, where Mrs Sediyapu showed us how to peel off the outer skin to reveal the soft, sticky tamarind. She then proceeded to remove the seeds in a wonderfully dexterous manner. Using as a dish the dried-out scoop from the base of a coconut frond (which we had seen at Satir's farm being used as hats), she took the mass of tamarind pulp in one hand and pressed it against a fierce-looking sickle held upturned with the other. The black seeds dropped like marbles into the palm-frond dish and a growing ball of de-seeded tamarind pulp filled her left hand. After a few days the tamarind pulp oxidises and turns black. The bulk of commercially produced tamarind is still hand-peeled this way, however it would be rare to find this degree of care being taken to remove the seeds.

The aroma of tamarind is vaguely fruity and sharp while the flavour is intensely acidic, tingling, refreshing and reminiscent of dried stone fruit. Tamarind is arguably the most popular souring agent in Indian cooking after lime or lemon. I like to make a refreshing soft drink by adding soda water and ice cubes to a tablespoon of tamarind water with a little sugar. Although it may seem moist, tamarind should never go mouldy as its high level of acidity acts as a preservative. Curry recipes will generally call for a quantity of tamarind water, typically 2 tablespoons to half a cup, to be added during cooking. To make tamarind water from the hard tamarind block, break off a walnut-sized piece (a 2 centimetre diameter ball) and put it into half a cup of hot water. Stir it around and worry it a bit with a spoon and leave for about 15 minutes. Strain off the liquid, squeezing the remaining pulp as dry as possible before discarding it. Tamarind water can be made in large batches and frozen in ice-cube trays to drop into cooking whenever the fruity tang of tamarind is required.

The long drive back to Mangalore in the late afternoon was tiring, yet the satisfaction at having seen and learnt so much, as well as the pleasure of meeting such hospitable people, made up for our weariness. The sleeper car on the Malabar Express was less comfortable than the journey to Mangalore. We arrived back in Kochi at 4.30 am, walked through the dark, empty streets to our apartment and slept well into the morning. It was now less than a week before we would have to leave India and we still had to travel upcountry into the cardamom hills.

WE MEET the CARDAMOM KING

Thampi called us to say that he had arranged for Palanichamy, one of his colleagues from the Spices Board, to accompany us into the cardamom hills, where we would see cardamom (*Eletaria cardamomum*) plantations, a cardamom auction and the Periyar wildlife sanctuary at Thekkady. After three weeks in dear old Kochi we were looking forward to getting up to the high country, where it would be a little cooler than down on the coast.

The day got off to a typical start with Palanichamy (pronounced 'Palliswarmy') and a driver arriving to collect us at nine in the morning instead of eight. A tall, good-looking man who considered himself to be a bit of a raconteur, we nicknamed him 'Pallis-smarmy'. He later confided that his secret ambition was to write romantic fiction. He suggested we visit a tea plantation at Munnar, north-east of Kochi, on our way to the cardamom hills. However when we mentioned how much we were looking forward to seeing the cardamom auction at Vandamettu, he said, 'Oh, that will be over by 12.30 so we'll miss it.' From our appalled silence Palanichamy gathered this was not good news, so he stopped at a Spices Board office and phoned to ask them to delay the proceedings as long as possible.

The driver stepped on the gas, no mean feat on these monsoon-washed roads. During the wet season, 3 metres of rain falls in these hills and one can only imagine the force of the torrents formed from the runoff. We turned onto a short cut that would bypass the tea plantation and hopefully get us to the auction sooner rather than later. The Ambassador stalwartly chugged up the steep winding road, the driver having to stop and change into first gear as we negotiated every hairpin bend. The agony of the climb, though, was almost compensated for by the beauty of the scenery. Each sharp, precipitous bend would reveal a tantalising vista of rolling, tropical hills seen through tall, vine-laced trees. Every now and then a far-off clearing would appear, and in it a large Portuguese-style church, sitting amongst the tangle of jungle like an apparition.

We passed through small villages with women fetching and carrying impossible loads while indolent youths and cigarette-smoking men sat idly passing the time of day. An Ambassador had been pushed off the road for repairs, a tarpaulin laid out on the ground beside it. Eight men were standing around the car with its bonnet up, and what looked like every greasy mechanical component from its engine bay was regurgitated all over the tarp. The men gazed contemplatively at the array of shafts, cogs, gears, piston rings, washers, brackets, ball bearings and hoses as if willing them to magically re-assemble themselves. I peered out the back window as we sped past in a cloud of dust, and wondered which head-scratching aspiring mechanic would make the first move.

As we drove into Vandamettu we could smell the distinct eucalyptus-like aroma of cardamom in the air. It was now 1.00 pm and the auction had just finished, but when we came into the auction room they good-naturedly put everything back in place and staged a dummy auction just for our benefit.

During the cardamom harvesting and drying season, auctions are held in many villages like this one. The auction room is about the size of a small classroom with tables and chairs lined around the walls facing the centre. In one morning forty or more lots may be put under the hammer, which could amount to 2 or 3 tonnes of cardamom pods. When a lot comes up, each of the buyers is given a sample of pods from that lot in a small plastic bag. He opens it and tips the cardamom into a dish and inspects the quality before bidding. The auctioneer stands in the middle and puts on a theatrical display of salesmanship in that inimitable fashion which is unique to this profession. A cacophony of shouts in Malayalam ring out, the bidding gets more and more excited as the price rises, and a buyer is nailed with a closure.

Quick as a wink the buyer, the price and the lot number are chalked up on the blackboard, the bowls of cardamom pods are tossed onto the red-carpeted floor and a new batch of bags is handed around. By the end of the auction, the discarded samples of peacock green pods are ankle deep on the floor. One could not be blamed for becoming light-headed as the astringent aroma tantalises the nostrils and clears the sinuses.

The auctioneer told us that some years ago the traders decided to sweep up the discarded lots of cardamom from the floor and sell them on the local market. The proceeds were then used to build a school. The practice has continued and the schools in the cardamom-growing areas benefit from this initiative, one that is particularly relevant in the state of Kerala, which claims to have the highest literacy rate in India.

We were really beginning to appreciate why the Indians call cardamom 'the queen of spices' (they refer to pepper as 'the king of spices'), and why it has been used since early Greek and Roman times. Cardamom will add a delicacy and freshness to curries like no other spice, and it complements sweets and fruits as well. Our next stop was the largest cardamom plantation in the south of India, owned by a man called Mr Jose, whom everyone refers to as 'The Cardamom King'.

The plantation looked like dense jungle, as cardamom is a perennial plant and it likes to grow in the canopy of shade provided by existing trees. For this reason, growers claim that cardamom is environmentally friendly, because the forest does not have to be cleared to grow the crop. Cardamom plants look a little like tall clumps of ginger without the flowers, with long, flat leaves that can grow up to a couple of metres tall.

What makes the plant unusual is that the flower stems grow out from the base around the perimeter of the clump, and the seed capsules, or pods as they are called when they are picked, form on these stems. Like so many spices, the pods are picked by hand, but instead of being dried in the sun, they are dried on shelving covered with wire mesh in a shed with a wire-mesh floor. When you peel away the paperbark-like pod, about ten tightly packed brown seeds are revealed.

Mr Jose, an urbane, quietly spoken man who commanded kingly obedience from his minions, took us to his drying shed, which was the size of two large houses. Under the shed is a furnace that is stoked all day and night to make the drying room hot, so that the pods dry within twenty-four hours to the most beautiful soft green colour, with a slightly shrivelled appearance. These are then cleaned to remove any remaining stems, and graded depending upon their colour, flavour, strength and size. Mr Jose took us to a large, fragrant room where about fifteen women were sitting cross-legged on the floor around a pile of cardamom pods about a metre high and over 2 metres wide. Each woman held a triangular, flat wicker tray with a few cupfuls of pods on it, and was rhythmically shaking them up into the air and catching them again, moving the tray with a slight forward and back movement, separating the waste from the good pods. These pods were then taken and bagged by workers standing behind the circle of women. There was something captivating about the fragrance of cardamom and the rustle of pods on woven trays sounding like a type of tambourine.

About thirty or more years ago, most cardamom pods were bleached to a very pale, almost cream colour, which was then considered desirable. However the Arabs were known to prefer their cardamom green, and it was considered a matter of great honour and prestige to be able to pass around the greenest cardamom when entertaining and partaking of their ritual coffee spiced with cardamom.

In the 1980s, Guatemala got the jump on India and became a major player in the world cardamom trade by supplying the greenest cardamom, thus attracting the very considerable Arab market. The situation suddenly changed and farmers strove to produce a really green dried cardamom pod. Most of the Indian cardamom you see now is very green and over the last ten years India has increased its share of the market considerably.

With all this talk of green cardamom pods, I must mention that there is another variety of cardamom called brown cardamom, black cardamom or large cardamom (*Cardamomum amomum*). These are about the size of a grape or small nutmeg, and have a soft, leathery pod concealing dark seeds just as the green one does. The flavour is pungent, with a rather odd smoky, camphor taste. I wouldn't use it as a substitute for green cardamom but some recipes will call for brown cardamom because of its distinctive flavour.

Cardamom always reminds me of the time, about thirty-five years ago, when my father bought a shipment of cardamom seeds from a Sri Lankan trader. When it arrived, he opened the neat wooden case lined with tin foil, and he was sure that amongst the cardamom seeds was a considerable amount of mice droppings. Now my father had been dealing mostly with herbs and some of the better known spices, and in those days cardamom was a rarity. The little seeds sometimes remained stuck together in segments and it is a shape that does look suspicious. As he wasn't exactly sure, he asked a relative of the trader who was living in Australia for advice. Dad was always very particular about quality, and he didn't want to take any chances.

Anyway, this fellow came out to have a look at the consignment of seeds. He pored over them, he looked at them closely, he rubbed them between his fingers, he smelt them and held them up to the light . . . then he tasted them. The first one went into his mouth, the seconds ticked away, he nibbled, gazed at the ceiling, called all his experienced taste buds and olfactory heritage to the fore and finally, after more dramatic tension than at a wine judging, pronounced, 'This is *not* a cardamom seed!'

This process was repeated three times before he announced with enthusiasm and excitement, mixed with a touch of due solemnity, '*This* is a cardamom seed!' Needless to say, Dad was extremely impressed with the analytical skills of our supplier's relative and his unselfish commitment to his trade. However, he sent the whole consignment back and only ever bought whole cardamom pods after that. Even the other day when I was adding cardamom seeds to some coffee, he wanted to see the pack of pods they came from.

We drove on to Myladumpara and the Indian Cardamom Research Institute (ICRI), which now comes under the auspices of the Spices Board. Like the Spices Research Station we visited in Ahmedabad, this research facility is focused on helping farmers find ways to improve quality and productivity. Again we found a lot of research on organic methods, more for economic reasons than big 'O' marketing rationales. One example was the use of a naturally occurring benign mould to fight another type of mould that attacks the rhizomes of cardamom plants, thereby obviating the need to use chemicals. We were also interested to learn that much of the research into growing vanilla in India was being conducted here and, although on a much smaller scale than in Mexico, some very good quality beans were being produced.

Our tour of the various laboratories complete, we felt we had seen enough beakers, pipettes, Bunsen burners, incubation chambers, negative pressure cabinets and gas chromatographs to last us for some time. It was getting late in the afternoon and Palanichamy took us over the road to the Spices Board guest-house where we would be staying the night. A 1970s solid, two-storey building, the design looked distinctly Russian, angular and utilitarian.

Our room was on the second floor and looked out into the treetops and over dense undergrowth, which was comprised almost entirely of cardamom. The evening air was light and cool and after a wash in cold water and a couple of gins laced with a squeeze of lime, we ate a simple meal of rice and dhal that had been prepared by the caretaker. We had developed a routine for coping with the rock-hard beds in many an Indian guesthouse. We would remove the two mattresses from the beds, put them on the floor on top of each other and then both sleep on the single-bed width, but double-thickness bed. Not so comfortable down on the steamy coast, but up here in the cool mountains, we snuggled up and slept like logs.

We expected that Palanichamy would have been out on the tiles that night with some of his local mates, but he was up bright-eyed and bushy-tailed the next morning and helped us polish off some more rice and dhal, followed by little sweet bananas, for breakfast. After an early morning stroll among the cardamom, we climbed back into the Ambassador with our overnight bags and headed to a resort that Mr Jose had built among some of his tea and cardamom plantations, called Carmellia. The name Carmellia is a word made up from combining cardamom and camellia (the family that tea bushes belong to).

Arriving at Carmellia was like finding an oasis of sophistication. Dotted among thickets of huge cardamom plants up to 3 metres high were neat, whitewashed, thick-walled cottages. In another part of the gardens, next to trimmed tea bushes, were honeymoon suites, small, round cottages with spiral stairways leading up to thatched lookouts on top. However, it would be hard to surpass the 'tree house', a stand-alone suite literally suspended up in the treetops. There was also the cave suite, the complete opposite, burrowed as it was claustrophobically underground. The gardens were immaculate but the icing on the cake was a turbaned old man wearing red and gold robes and sporting a white handlebar moustache, who was wandering around playing a wooden flute.

Before we departed, Mr Jose showed us his tea factory where we saw just what is involved in transforming some innocent green leaves into the beverage that sustained an empire. Tea plantations are an extraordinary sight when one first sees them. Whole hillsides of green appear to be perfectly manicured, as every tea bush is handpicked to the same height. Tea pickers' tracks meander through the bushes, making it look like a gigantic, impossible jigsaw.

The top floor of the tea factory is made of wooden slats, and when we visited, the whole area was covered with leaves that had been picked a couple of days earlier and were partially drying down to about a 40 per cent moisture content. The next stage involves pushing these leaves down a chute into a machine that rolls them for up to thirty minutes. This rubbing activates enzymes in the leaves which are a critical element in creating the familiar taste of black leaf tea. The rolled leaves are then left in piles where they continue to oxidise and develop more flavour. Some people refer to this stage as fermenting but Mr Jose's factory manager went to pains to explain that the leaves are not really fermenting, because unlike this oxidation reaction, fermentation typically refers to the actions of yeasts and sugars. The darkened piles of rubbed and chopped leaves are then dried to 12 per cent moisture in kilns at 400 degrees centigrade before final grading and boxing for sale.

By now we were on the eastern side of Kerala, in the district known as Idukki, and were heading due south to a little town called Kumily, which is just 4 kilometres from Thekkady and the entrance to the Periyar wildlife park. Kumily is a charming little town full of Kashmiri-owned curio and spice shops. It is the home of the Spice Village resort, where thatched-roof cabins are dotted amongst pepper vines, nutmeg and clove trees and the swimming pool is shaded by an enormous tamarind tree. You can see why tourists are so drawn to Kumily – it has all the atmosphere of an Indian town but is small enough to feel non-threatening and comfortable.

Late afternoon is the best time of day to go to the Periyar wildlife sanctuary and Palanichamy had arranged for us to take a lake cruise. The sanctuary of over 700 square kilometres surrounds a 26 square kilometre lake that was created by the British in 1895. It is a popular tourist attraction and, if one is fortunate, antelopes, bison, wild boar, and elephants can be seen. They also claim to have about thirty-five tigers, but after four trips to Periyar, I have not seen one yet.

When we arrived at the departure point for the boats there was a group of about thirty schoolchildren who were quite fascinated by us and before long they had all gathered around and were wanting to know our names. Finally one mischievous little girl plucked up enough courage to touch Liz, who then shook hands with her. They were so interested to find out what we felt like that before long we were shaking hands with all of them.

The boat Thampi had arranged for us was about 10 metres long with a half-enclosed cabin, like a miniature ferry, and a fumy diesel engine positioned amidships. As it chugged rhythmically amongst the long-drowned trees on the artificial lake venturing up little estuaries in search of wildlife I couldn't help thinking of the *African Queen*. The boat driver had very sharp eyes and pointed out turtles, kingfishers as they flashed past in a blue streak, deer twitchily grazing, and nesting cormorants. We saw some wild boar, ugly things, and continued to chug along as the afternoon sun sank below the hills and the chance of seeing elephants increased.

In an open grassy area, in the shade and near the water's edge we saw a group of five elephants – four adults and one a little over a year old. Liz, who has been an elephant lover and collector of elephant memorabilia for years, was thrilled at the sight of these noble creatures in their natural habitat.

Dinner at the Spice Village was sumptuous to say the least. What onerous decisions one has make on such occasions. How much tomato and garlic rasam should I ladle over my pile of fluffy Kerala rice? Will I have fish *moilee* or a Kerala fish curry? Then perhaps I should be content with some chicken pepper masala and snack on Kerala chicken kebabs with naan bread. No, I think I'll go for the *kozhy varutharacha* curry (chicken curry), *avial* (mixed vegetables in a mild curry gravy) and *pachadi* (pumpkin in a yoghurt-based sauce). These were accompanied by garlic pickle, deep fried white (curd) chillies, and a sweet ginger pickle. For dessert I had *payasam*, a vermicelli, milk, raisin, cashew nut, sugar and cardamom dish that resembles a sweet, runny rice pudding. The masala tea was spiced with lemongrass, cinnamon quills and cardamom pods. All this food reminded me of a story my mother-in-law told me about one of her brothers when he was little. After an enormous Christmas dinner he said to his father, 'Please carry me to bed, but don't bend me.' Liz and I just managed to waddle to our bungalow, and slept soundly among the pepper vines, plots of lemongrass, cardamom shrubs and nutmeg and clove trees.

We were able to return to Kochi via Munnar, as we had no cardamom-auction-enforced time restraints. Munnar is a hill station town north of Vandametta and is famous for its magnificent undulating slopes and hills draped in a verdant carpet of tea plantations. We were just drawing into the outskirts of the town when we saw a procession of thirty or more young women, dressed in the most brightly coloured saris. Each one was carrying a basket of what looked like bean sprouts on her head, and one by one the baskets were being placed on the back of a truck. Palanichamy explained that all these people are workers from the adjoining state, Tamil Nadu, and what we were witnessing was a ritual that was part of the festivals at this time of year. Young women of marriageable age plant sprouts and wheat in a basket about twenty days before the ceremony. The vigour of the sprouts is an indication of the prosperity for that young woman's family for the next year, and an indication of her potential fecundity. When the truck was loaded with all the baskets the smiling, bright-eyed, beautiful young women had brought to it, everyone clambered on board and the baskets were taken up to the temple.

The rest of the eight-hour drive home to Kochi the next day was punctuated with stops to talk to pepper farmers by the roadside, breaks to have a cool drink and, of course, lunch. After the previous night's dinner we thought we would never need to eat again. However, when Palanichamy suggested stopping at the Indian Government Idukki Tourist office for lunch we realised how much we loved our food. In very basic, canteen-style surroundings we had a delicious lunch of Kerala rice, sambar and vegetables.

Our month in the south of India nearly over, we felt ready to get back to Australia and continue making plans for our shop, which we hoped to open within six months. We were brimming with ideas for our next Spice Discovery Tour and although we had seen a lot of India, we found ourselves painfully aware of just how many more interesting things there are to experience on the subcontinent.

We put on a little farewell dinner at the Avenue Regent (it was the least we could do after spending the last month popping in and out and availing ourselves of their air-conditioning) and thanked many of the people who had been so hospitable during our stay.

LUNCH on the BANKS
of the EUPHRATES

By early 1999 our shop had been open for eighteen months, I had begun writing my first book, *Spice Notes*, and Liz and I were becoming increasingly fascinated with the spice sumac (*Rhus coriaria*). We had learnt a little about this much-used Middle Eastern spice about ten years earlier when we both contributed a section on herbs and spices to a book called *What Food is That?* At the time we were surprised to discover that the purple powder we had seen sprinkled over the onion rings in doner kebab outlets was sumac, a tangy, fruity, lemon-like spice. My uneasiness about the relationship of this variety of rhus tree to the poisonous rhus trees had never been fully satiated. The sumac tree, which bears berries for culinary use, is one of around 150 varieties of rhus tree, many of which are recorded as causing severe skin irritation and poisoning. The decorative rhus trees, whose leaves turn a striking bright red in autumn, are declared noxious in Australia. One of the women working for us at Somerset Cottage in the 1980s came to work one day with the most extreme allergic reaction I have ever seen. She had been cutting back a rhus tree at her home over the weekend and every inch of skin that could be seen was bright red and horribly inflamed. The image of her reaction to the rhus tree has stayed in my consciousness ever since.

Knowing that Turkey was a major producer of sumac, we decided to go there in search of the farms where it is grown. A bonus would be the opportunity to see the famous spice merchants of Istanbul.

I recalled that an Australian who had worked in the spice trade for a number of years had moved to Turkey. I had first met Craig Semple at a Spice Association meeting about nine years before and knowing that sumac was grown in Turkey, directed my first line of enquiry to Craig. Tracking him down was not difficult as he was active in exporting Turkish produce to Australia and one of the traders gave me his contact details.

Over the next couple of months we spent our free time poring over maps of Turkey as Craig emailed details of the areas where sumac is grown and processed. Fortunately we had chosen exactly the right time of year for this trip – July. As we looked at place names such as Gaziantep, Nizip and Cappadocia all the pre-travel anticipation began to ferment in our veins. Our travel agent, Ossie Pitts, started on the case. Due to the limited time we had available for travelling and our woeful lack of any other language, Ossie recommended an English-speaking guide who would also be our driver when we were in the south-east of the country. Craig had arranged for a representative of Belmar, a Turkish trading company, to meet us in Gaziantep and take us to the sumac-growing area. Craig suggested we fly direct to Istanbul, visit the famous spice markets and take in some sightseeing before flying to Gaziantep.

We arrived in Istanbul, formerly Constantinople and in the mists of time, historic Byzantium, at seven in the morning. After over twenty hours travelling and little chance for sleep in economy class, the sensible thing to do would have been to rest. However after a shower and change of clothes we ate a delicious breakfast of figs, plums and apricots poached in syrup and hit the streets. The driver who had picked us up from the airport had offered to collect us later and be our guide. We wondered how a guide who spoke very little English would be any use to us, but as we were not meeting our arranged guide until arriving in Gaziantep, we decided to give him a go. Sheriff collected us at 10.00 am and drove us to the Blue Mosque, Sultan Ahmet Camii, and said he would be back at four o'clock. Liz and I gazed blankly at each other and said in unison, 'Some guide!' A carpet salesman accosted us, and being the first person we had met who spoke good English, nearly became our de facto guide until we shook him off. We imagined that after an hour of his genial hospitality, the pressure to buy a carpet in gratitude for his help would be irresistible.

Currency always takes some getting used to when you arrive, and parting with 5 million lire to gain entrance to the Hagia Sophia was a bit of a shock until we calculated that it equalled about A$20. We were to discover that entry fees applied to nearly everything here and in one day you could easily part with a hundred dollars. Initial resentment at the 'milk the tourist' strategy gave way to a realisation that any contribution towards the upkeep and restoration of historic sites is readily justified and should not be begrudged. As we entered the basilica we wondered what all the fuss was about, until we ascended into the main dome and were bathed in the reflected light of millions of gold mosaic tiles.

On the way out we were approached by a well-spoken gentleman who offered to guide us for the rest of the day. Roaming around until 4.00 pm with our Lonely Planet guidebook (useful as it is) could not be as rewarding as having some human help, so we struck a deal at five million lire for the afternoon. Cengiz (pronounced Genghis as in Genghis Khan) was a retired architect and said he liked working as a tourist guide as it gives him a chance to pass on his vast local knowledge.

Istanbul was full of atmosphere, names like Bosporus, Ottoman, Sultanahmet district, Golden Horn and Topkapi Palace conjuring up a library of images and tales that until now we had only read about. Cengiz tutored us with a decidedly architectural bent, much of which was lost on us in our somewhat jetlagged state. The next site we explored was the Basilica Cistern, basically an enormous underground water storage tank, 70 metres wide and 140 metres long, built in AD 532 by the Emperor Justinian the Great. There is only a small amount of water left in the Basilica Cistern now. The 336 columns used in its construction were the leftover columns brought from other sites that had been demolished to build the Hagia Sophia. Walking among the huge columns supporting the roof and hearing the sound of dripping water echoing all around felt quite eerie. But we welcomed the cool atmosphere after the mid-thirty degree heat outside.

Because the columns had been transported from demolished buildings (it still amazes me how they managed to move them), they were in many different styles and shapes. Cengiz showed us two columns with the most beautifully carved heads at their bases. I found it quite incredible that these details could be hidden away in a storage tank. At one end of the Cistern was a candle-lit coffee shop where we could have sat for an hour or so and contemplated Justinian's rule one thousand five hundred years ago. However a guide in tow does not go with romantic situations, so we decided to be contemplative somewhere else when it would be just the two of us.

Early afternoon and lunch beckoned. Cengiz took us to a restaurant where we ordered a grilled eggplant dish and dolmas (rice and mince wrapped in vine leaves), which Liz adored and I felt could do with a little spice. After lunch we walked to the Archaeological Museum – a visit that would have been far less enlightening without a guide. The main item of interest among the early Greek, Hellenistic and Roman marbles and bronzes on display was a sarcophagus with the grisly skeleton of its former inhabitant in a glass case beside it. Marble tombs also on display were covered in intricate carvings of battle scenes, with life-like veins protruding on horses' heads, their hocks, cannon-bones and tendons standing out from the exertion of the fight.

Our next stop was the Spice Bazaar, or the Egyptian Market as it is sometimes called. Istanbul is divided by the Bosporus, the body of water flowing between the Black Sea and the Sea of Marmara. The west side, where the Old City and the majority of historic sites are situated, is known as European Istanbul. This is divided by an inlet of the Bosporus referred to as the Golden Horn, named for its shape and the colour the water turns at sunset. The eastern side of the Bosporus is referred to as Asian Istanbul and rows of charming two- and three-storey weatherboard houses line the river's shores.

The Spice Bazaar is at the northern end of the maze of undercover shopfronts and streets that constitute the Grand Bazaar, which is on the 'European' side of the Bosporus. A teeming congregation of traders in many mysterious alleyways, the Grand Bazaar has grown continually since the mid-fifteenth century, and is one of the city's most popular tourist attractions. Some of our well-travelled customers had waxed lyrical about these markets in Istanbul where you can buy a vast array of spices, such as saffron (*Crocus sativus*), for a fraction of the cost they sell for in Australia.

My first reaction to the dozen or so spice shops clustered here was to give them ten out of ten for presentation and atmosphere. At the front were large bags with neatly rolled 'bobbysocks' rims overflowing with whole red chillies, onions, garlic and dried figs. Tiered behind were containers piled high with brightly coloured cones of coriander, cumin, chilli powder, sumac and peppercorns. For quality and value I would give them about four out of ten. One trader was selling allspice berries that were so old I did not recognise them at first and cubebs (*Piper cubeba*) absolutely devoid of flavour. All in all there were about twenty different herbs and spices on display but the saffron scam was a classic.

Saffron is the world's most expensive spice and is often said to be worth its weight in gold. It is the stigma from an autumn-flowering crocus and because there are only three stigmas per flower, the yield is very low. In fact it takes about 5000 threads to make up just 25 grams. A farmer with 2 hectares of saffron might be lucky enough in a good year to be able to fill both hands with his annual production. No wonder the real thing is so costly.

While the bouquet, flavour strength and colour of saffron will vary depending upon its country of origin and the quality, saffron is best described as having a woody, honey-like, oaked-wine, tenacious aroma and a bitter, lingering, appetite-stimulating taste. Its pungent aroma comes from a substance called safranal and the earthy, bittersweet flavour comes from another substance, picrocrocin. Some grades of saffron can contain a percentage of pale yellow styles, which although lacking the colouring strength of the stigmas, still manage to impart a classic saffron taste. The style joins the stigmas into the base of the flower and has a saffron flavour but little colour content. The most treasured component of saffron is its powerful, water-soluble dye crocin, a natural colourant held within the blood-red stigmas. When released, saffron tints like nothing else; it is as if pure sunshine had been magically infused to create the orange-yellow of the first light of day.

Most of the traders were selling reasonably good Iranian saffron which, after prolonged haggling, worked out at about A$5 a gram. It contained a proportion of pale yellow styles along with the deep red stigmas. Saffron with style included should be up to 20 per cent cheaper than pure stigmas. The majority of the shops were doing a roaring trade in turmeric or, as they called it, Indian saffron. We thought, though, that the *pièce de résistance* was the Turkish saffron and we recognised this as the one that draws the tourists in. When it comes to buying saffron there is no creature more gullible than the enthusiastic tourist, haggling over piles of golden-yellow strands in the spice markets of Istanbul, or for that matter in any other exotic location. I was most amused, and proud, when Liz fixed her eye on a trader spruiking his 'real Turkish saffron', which was actually safflower (*Carthamus tinctorius*). She said to him with an icy gaze, 'That's not saffron,' to which he replied, 'Of course it's not,' and continued shouting to the unaware, 'Real saffron, real Turkish saffron!' After this incident we found most of the traders less than co-operative, obviously a bit affronted by our smart-ass assessment of their wares. One trader, however, did show me something very clever in the world of fake saffron, and that was a selection of extruded, miniature, jelly-snake-like strands the shape of saffron stigmas. The colour was a darker red than the real spice, but these strands were impregnated with an aroma distinctly similar to saffron. My guess is that they were made of coloured and flavoured gelatin. It would be interesting to know how many buyers have been taken in by this brilliant yet simple piece of alchemy.

Before we get too purist about the spice traders of Istanbul, I have seen safflower on sale in Australia labelled as saffron. The more reputable merchants put the names *kasubha* or *casubha*, under the heading 'saffron' as that is what safflower is called in India and the Philippines respectively. Although the colour is less golden and there is no similarity in flavour between safflower and saffron, safflower has become a useful natural colouring alternative to the potentially allergic artificial colours Tartrazine E102 and Sunset Yellow E110.

We walked further until we came into the covered bazaar that, according to Cengiz, held over 4000 little shops trading in almost every imaginable variety of merchandise. Jewellery, plates, clothes, souvenirs, leather bags, antiques, old coins, stamps, you name it, it was here. On the way we witnessed a little family drama where a middle-aged woman was throwing a tantrum and screaming at the top of her voice in the crowded street. Shoppers had stopped to take in this domestic scene – mother clad in black, sweat running profusely from a brow formed by years of worried parenting. Heavy, dimpled arms flung about in heated exasperation. Her pouting, smooth-skinned daughter, stood languid in tight, round-bottom-hugging jeans and teetering high heels. Cengiz translated the scene for us. Mother was in the market for a wedding dress for her daughter and the one she had chosen was more expensive than she'd expected! As parents of three daughters we said to each other, 'So what's new?'

As we walked through the pets and the garden section of the market we were amused to come across a stall displaying open bags of sumac, paprika and birdseed right beside the open bags of naphthalene flakes and rat poison. Needless to say we refrained from making any culinary purchases there. Doubling back past our favourite spice marketers we walked over the bridge that straddles the Golden Horn and took the underground tram that was built in the late 1800s. This ingenious contraption works on a counterbalancing system whereby two carriages are connected to a cable. As one carriage goes down the hill its weight pulls the other one up, then vice versa. The journey of a couple of kilometres up a steep hill takes one and a half minutes, very convenient and much better than walking after a day's continual ambling.

We loved the atmosphere in Istanbul and as evening came on we watched the sun setting on the Golden Horn. Every hill and slope seemed to have a domed and minareted mosque that was at first silhouetted against the afternoon sun and then lit by a full moon. They were bathed in cool evening light as the incantation of calling-to-prayer echoed from loud-speakers attached to minarets across the city. Two weeks later this beautiful city and its colourful inhabitants were to be rocked by the worst earthquake in its history.

As we strolled through lanes and alleys that reminded us uncannily of the winding streets of Toledo in Spain, we came to a small restaurant which looked like no more than a shop window. In the window for all passers-by to see was a woman in traditional, peasant dress, sitting with a cloth spread over her out-stretched legs, making pancakes. She was rolling them out with a rolling pin no thicker than a piece of dowel, on a small, low round table. Nimble, experienced hands transferred these pancakes to a gas hotplate beside her, then she added the cooked ones to a neat, growing pile. We couldn't resist going inside. The owner showed us to a table, took some of the pancakes, wrapped them around spinach and salty cheese and served us dinner. Our first thoughts were, This will be interesting, but we can find somewhere later to have a proper meal. Such thoughts were dispelled by the time we were two-thirds through our pancakes. Simple and basic, the meal of pide was tasty and was also incredibly satisfying. After the meal we resisted the 'keep you awake for twenty-four hours' Turkish coffee and went back to the hotel on our tired feet and booked a wake-up call for 4.00 am.

The flight to Ankara and the connecting flight to Gaziantep were comfortable and uneventful. There had been some problems with terrorists so security dictated that all pas-sengers identify their bags on the tarmac. All unidentified ones stayed there. How naïve these measures now seem, in the wake of September 11.

We were met at the airport by the guide Ossie had booked for us, a portly, silver-haired gentlemen in a suit and tie. He introduced himself as Net, short for Necdet, and escorted us to his beautifully kept, air-conditioned diesel Mercedes. Gaziantep had all the elements of a purpose-built city and not a lot of physical charm. Every building appeared to be cement grey with lots of off-the-form concrete, more as a result of practicality rather than some trendy architect's fancy. The hotel sported metres of dark red carpet and when we got to our spartan but comfortable room, we were amused by the violently pinky-purple Formica lining the window recesses. Growing outside the hotel was a beautiful hedge of rosemary (*Rosmarinus officinalis*). When we commented on it to the staff we were astounded that no one seemed to know of its use with lamb. We found that every meal involved meat, which was more often than not lamb, and sometimes substantial quantities, so to have a herb which complements lamb so well and not appreciate it seemed to be an awful waste.

Settled in and unpacked by 10.00 am, we went down to the foyer and took little glasses of hot apple tea. Apple tea is offered by every carpet seller who wants to have an excuse to delay you while showing off his wares. It tastes just like clear apple juice that has been warmed and is often made by infusing pieces of dried apple in a teapot. We met Craig's friend from Izmir, Halit, who was accompanied by Ibrihim, a tall, good-looking chap whom Liz found swarthily attractive, and Ibrihim's old, stubble-chinned, cracked and nicotine-toothed, smiling uncle. None of them spoke a word of English so Net acted as interpreter, a role he revelled in. This was not just taking a couple of tourists around the sights of outback Turkey, he was talking business with his countrymen and adding even more knowledge to his encyclopaedic mind. With tea over we set off for Ibrihim and his uncle's farm at Nizip; the purpose of our mission was to see a grove of sumac trees.

The landscape was rugged and barren. Fawn, stony ground appeared to be just waiting for water to transform it into lush fields, or support fruitful olive, walnut and pistachio groves under the Anatolian sun. The orchard of sumac trees was haphazard as if the trees had grown up at random, rather than being planted in ordered rows. I leapt from the car and trudged through the dusty field towards my quarry – a mature 3 metre high, female sumac tree laden with ripe berries. The branches and dense frond-like foliage had a diameter of about 2 metres, giving it a neat, globe-like appearance. Although deciduous, Ibrihim assured us that the leaves never turn bright scarlet, as other rhus trees do, and he has never known anyone to suffer an allergic reaction from contact with the leaves or fruits.

The sumac berries stood out from the foliage like Christmas decorations, tightly bunched in conical-shaped clusters 8 to 10 centimetres long and about 2 centimetres across at the widest point near the base. The edible clusters droop like bunches of grapes, while the poisonous ones sit up like pyramid-shaped candles. Each berry, which develops from a similarly dense bunch of small white flowers, is a little larger than a peppercorn. When fully formed it is green and covered with hairy down like a kiwifruit. Most of the non-poisonous varieties of rhus trees have hairy berries, whereas the fruits on decorative types are smooth. The berries then ripen to a pinkish red and are finally deep crimson when harvested. Sumac berries have a very thin outer skin and flesh surrounding an extremely hard, tick-shaped seed. There were a few male trees among the grove – they do not bear fruit, but the leaves are harvested and added to ground sumac spice or mixed with thyme and oregano to make a kind of *za'atar*. *Za'atar* is a traditional Middle Eastern mixture of thyme, toasted sesame seeds, sumac and salt, and is delicious when sprinkled on oiled flatbread and toasted.

Before heading off to the processing factory Ibrihim's uncle took me across a field of spearmint (*Mentha spicata*) to a grove of walnut trees. The mint field, which was by a river, covered two lush hectares and was irrigated. The mint was pungently refreshing underfoot, as our tread crushed its oil cells and released its fragrant perfume into the dry, warm air. Spearmint takes on a unique, subtle flavour and various aromatic characteristics depending upon the soil and climatic conditions it is growing in. To my mind, Turkish spearmint is the most heavenly mint I have encountered, and we could not resist importing it for our shop. At the walnut grove Ibrihim's uncle cut open some fresh walnuts for me to taste. I did not know they could be eaten like this and quite liked the lack of sharpness compared to the dry nuts.

Afterwards, Net ushered me back into the car to drive us to the sumac processing plant where Halit buys his sumac. At the factory, Ibrihim and his uncle introduced us to his four workers. The men were in their late fifties with lots of grey stubble and little Muslim caps covering thinning, white hair. Net was now in a flurry of translation as Halit explained the sumac trade. Ibrihim and Uncle expounded upon the ins and outs of processing and the workers proudly showed off their work.

The clusters of harvested berries are dried in the sun for

a couple of days before processing. This involves putting the clusters in a stone mill, an amazing contraption in itself. Imagine two large round stones, about the size of truck tyres, joined by an axle half a metre long. A shaft comes up from the bottom of what looks like a giant washing machine tub, and joins to the centre of the axle. The clusters are crushed by the wheels, turning at only about ten revolutions per minute, until most of the red, acidic flesh has been pummelled, crushed and smeared from its hold on the tiny, light brown seeds.

The next stage is to shovel a barrowload of these crushings onto a rectangular vibrating sieve, 2 metres long and 1 metre wide. The material that falls through the sieve is the best quality and it is deep crimson, fruity and acidic. The acid taste comes from malic acid (the same acid as in sour apples) contained in the downy hairs on the berries. The pieces of sumac, stem and seeds that remain in the sieve are returned to the mill for further crushing and re-sieving. The rock-hard little seeds that are not pulverised in the mill are ground in a separate grinder to yield a coarse, pale yellow powder. Different grades of sumac are produced by mixing various proportions of ground seeds to crushed sumac flesh, making a product that is lighter in colour and less tangy. The better grades contain much less powdered seed than the lower grades. It is a common practice to use the leaves from the male trees as another means of diluting sumac with a low-cost ingredient. Finally salt is added to the sumac to help it retain its colour, and to enhance the acidic flavour. Sometimes sumac is 'finished' by mixing in cottonseed oil to make it darker and shinier.

On the way out of the factory we saw a load of 'Turkish saffron' (safflower petals) being delivered from nearby farms, and we had a good laugh with our new friends about the spice markets in Istanbul trying to pass it off as real saffron.

After our sumac experience, we all went for lunch in a small town nearby called Birecik, on the banks of the Euphrates. The restaurant was in the open with shady awnings, trees and a splendid view across the fast-running river and pock-marked cliffs, honeycombed with caves and remnants of a Roman wall. The specialty was local fish, quite oily and a bit too strong for our liking. However we enjoyed just sitting there listening to people speaking in a language we couldn't understand. Net would translate the things he thought were of interest to us while we soaked up the atmosphere. We felt a sense of history as we looked across the Euphrates to a wall two thousand years old.

Eventually we parted company with our hosts when Halit had to fly back to his office in Izmir. We were delighted some months later, when we received our first shipment of sumac from Turkey, to know we had seen the trees it grew on and the factory where it was processed. When we opened the bags and smelt the fruity, tangy aroma we were transported back to Nizip, the little factory with its old men and the whole wonderful experience of being fortunate enough to have visited there.

That evening we took a short stroll around Gaziantep. Net had told us that the town was famous for its baklava, and we found a beautiful shop dedicated to baklava and pistachio logs. The pistachio logs looked like strips of bright green plasticine, and tasted so sweet and indulgent that we couldn't resist buying some to go with our baklava.

We made our way back to the hotel and dined on a

selection of red meats cooked on skewers and served with lettuce and tomato salad. We had to ask for sumac to dress it,
though. Net kept us entertained with little stories at which he
laughed uproariously, obviously understanding the funnier elements a little better than we did. Net is a devout Muslim and
we found it interesting to learn that as a guide he specialises in
taking Christian groups on tours of the Holy Land. His knowledge of the Bible would put the average Christian to shame.

The drive the following day from Gaziantep to
Cappadocia was a long one, taking many hours. The roads were
better than we expected and Net was keen to push the
Mercedes up to 160 kilometres per hour whenever he got the
chance. The landscape reminded me of western New South
Wales with long stretches of flat grasslands broken by low hills
and crossings over dry riverbeds, interspersed with pockets of
vegetation and small farms. After heading inland from Adana
to buy apricots from a roadside stall we stopped at the top of a
long, steep climb north-west of Gaziantep. Net warned us to be
careful of the wind which blows so strongly up here. I realised
he wasn't joking when I had to use all my strength to push the
car door open against its force. More like a gale, it was cool and
a pleasant relief from the heat around Aksaray, Nigde and
Tarsus, towns we'd passed on our way from Gaziantep.

By late afternoon we arrived in Nevşehir and collected a
rock and took a photo. The reason for this little ritual was to
bring back a memento for a friend's mother-in-law. Tess Mallos
has written a number of books on Middle Eastern cooking and
is one of Australia's foremost experts on the subject. One hot
Sunday Sydney afternoon, she and her husband John kindly
brought around a tub containing her orange blossom ice-cream

and the recipe for making it. The consistency and delicate flavour were like nothing I had tasted before and it is included in *Spice Notes* in the chapter on mastic. John's mother's family was moved out of Nevşehir in 1924 as part of the process of ethnic cleansing which was happening at the time. We washed the rock thoroughly and fortunately customs allowed us to bring it back into Australia.

Net took us to see some of the sights of Cappadocia before dark. It is a place that almost defies description. The extraordinary shapes of the landscape range from toadstool-shaped towers to fanciful Santa's-elves peaked caps. All kinds of moonscape-like features abound, and it looked as though they would have hobgoblins, pixies, fairies, elves and all manner of weird and fanciful life forms inhabiting them.

These mystical rock formations, made from soft volcanic ash, have been shaped by millions of years of erosion, followed by man's burrowing and excavations to form an ants' nest of human habitation. In these labyrinths of rock, ordered cities were created with schools, places of worship, cooking areas and myriad hiding places to protect the occupants, mostly Christians, from their enemies.

The hotel in the town of Avanos was at the low end of four star. We had a tiny room with very firm single beds, and the window was large but there was no through-breeze to give relief from the 35 degree Celsius temperature. Dinner was mostly meat, unspiced and served with a crisp, fresh salad. We now made a point of requesting sumac to sprinkle on our salads, and although we tried every possible pronunciation – *soomach*, *soomack* and even *smak* – the waiters would wait for Net's confirmation that these two Australians really knew what they wanted. He became quite garrulous as we were now comfortable in each other's company and the effects of the raki, an anise-flavoured alcoholic drink similar to ouzo and pastis, were taking effect. Net liked to have his raki brought in a small glass, to which he would add a couple of measures of water, turning the fragrant, pungent, clear liquid cloudy.

Breakfast was basic: orange cordial, hard-boiled eggs, cold meats, cheese, firm bread and more flies than you get at an Aussie barbecue. Net murmured his prayers as the car's diesel engine warmed up and the air-conditioning cooled the interior, then off we set for a day of exploring Cappadocia. Our first destination was the underground city where the Christians hid from the Romans some two thousand years ago. We arrived at what looked like a little settlement with a couple of shops in the middle of nowhere. It was actually the entrance. Fees paid, Net remained on the surface while Liz and I explored underground. We learnt that the entire city, which accommodated thousands of inhabitants at one time, was burrowed out of the rock, utilising existing caves and sinkholes. The tunnels went down for six levels and although they were narrow, and some so low that one had to bend right over to walk through them, they did not feel claustrophobic. The first galleries close to the surface were where the livestock were kept. Other sections were used for cooking, schooling, sleeping and chapels for prayers. Another city 10 kilometres away was once connected to this settlement by a tunnel. These cities contained about 10,000 people and were protected by huge 'Indiana Jones' style circular stone doors a metre and a half in diameter. These round doors could be rolled across the entrances making it impossible for the Romans to get in. After nearly an hour of meandering in a semi-crouched position through galleries and up and down steps carved in the rock, our backs were aching and it was time to move on.

Back on our journey around Cappadocia we stopped at the Valley of Pigeons, so named because the people who had made their homes in the caves carved pigeon cotes in the rock walls. I'm not entirely sure of their purpose, perhaps they helped to disguise the evidence of human habitation or the pigeons may have been good for eating. Like a child, I enjoyed clambering up ladders and going into cubbyholes and caves, which either felt incredibly secluded or gave panoramic views from windows in the rock peepholes.

On our way into Göreme we passed apricot orchards with trees so laden with fruit that the branches were propped up to prevent them from breaking. As we got out of the car to take a closer look, a young girl near the roadside greeted us and took us deeper into the orchard where an old couple, probably her grandparents, were laying halved apricots out on plastic sheets in the sun to dry. The grandfather took great pride in showing us his trees and gave us some dried apricots to taste. When our daughters were little, we always called dried apricots 'ears' because of their similarity to that part of one's anatomy. We thought these ears were the best we had ever tasted and after passing suitably complimentary comments about the fresh and dried apricots we bade them goodbye. The old man would not let us go without taking a bag each of fresh and dried fruit. He would not hear of us paying for them, but finally Net convinced him to accept some payment in token for our appreciation and 'to put towards the little girl's education'.

Having seen The Phallic Forest, which resembles a

Stonehenge of penises, with dozens of tourist stalls selling kitsch models, we went on to Göreme in the hope of meeting the owner of Indigo Gallery, Ruth Lockwood. Her name had been given to us as we waited for a taxi to take us from our shop in Sydney to the airport. A customer had noticed our bags, and hearing we were going to Turkey, she told us she knew an Australian who had a carpet shop and guesthouse in Göreme, so naturally we decided to look her up. We'd studiously avoided the carpet sellers of Istanbul and all approaches made to flog us a rug were fended off with icy, non-purchasing determination. So when we met Ruth we had in the back of our minds that we might buy something for the living room above the shop in Rozelle. Net asked around some contacts and we found Ruth's shop with no problems.

Our first impression was that Indigo Gallery was a carpet version of Herbie's Spices. We drank apple tea and for two hours Ruth explained the intricacies of carpet making, why the quality varies and lots of interesting soft-sell facts that really do get you in. Until now we had not been aware that many of the rugs sold are old and much of their value is attributed to the individuality and styles of the nomadic women who made them. To the uninitiated, most of the carpets looked the same, however, once your attention is drawn to the unique quirks of each maker you look at the rugs in a completely different way.

We ended up buying a kilim in a 'sumak' weave and a quirky rug that was about forty years old and made from a camel saddlebag that will always remind us of Cappadocia.

Loaded up with our carpets and their certificates of authenticity from Ruth, we parted like old friends and headed off to do more sightseeing before going to dinner at an underground restaurant owned by a friend of Net's. We know every guide we use anywhere in the world gets kickbacks from the restaurants, traders and shops they bring their hapless victims to. It is all part of the game, and as long as we're not being fleeced or misled, Liz and I don't have a problem with it. Before dinner we sat in deck chairs near the restaurant, the sun setting behind us, casting long shadows across the Cappadocian valley. We drank a few cooling ales and Net was uncharacteristically contemplative, nursing his raki and giving us the chance to quietly absorb the wonder of this extraordinary place.

The restaurant was carved out of the rock in a large circular design with a big, round dance floor. The floorshow consisted of five men and four women performing various folk dances. Music was provided by a drummer and a clarinet player, the musicians sounding more like four players than two. The whole space echoed and reverberated to their enthusiastic performance as an attractive young belly dancer entered to wild acclaim from a number of American GIs in the audience.

The dancer selected about seven blokes from the audience, yours truly included, and proceeded to give us belly dancing lessons. Then to my horror, and everyone's ribald amusement, she removed our shirts for a display of our newly acquired skill. Luckily Liz was without the camera, so the whole event can go down in family folklore without any photographic evidence!

The next morning we headed towards Izmir, once the Hellenistic city-state of Smyrna, 400 kilometres away on the west coast. We knew Net wanted to get us to Izmir before dark, so we were reluctant to ask him to stop at the sites along the way. Throughout Turkey there are sites that may have been the remains of destroyed churches or ruins of long-forgotten *cara-vanserai*. The *caravanserai* were walled structures built as resting places for groups of medieval travelling merchants. The thick walls, courtyards and stables would allow the travellers with their cargo to rest in safety. Often we'd pass a blur of rocks and Net would exclaim, '*Caravanserai!*' Finally we stopped at a large *caravanserai* at Afyon. The four main stone walls were at least 6 metres high, imposing and clearly sufficient to keep marauding bandits at bay. Inside were well-laid-out ablutions areas, a large courtyard and an enormous covered stable for camels and live-stock. Huge columns nearly a metre wide supported the arched roof. In the dark coolness of this vast space, we could imagine the hubbub, smells of animals and cooking fires, as camel trains laden with precious spices from the east made their way to ancient cities such as Ephesus on the Aegean sea.

It was mid afternoon by the time we had lunch at a tourist-cum-truck stop. An entrepreneurial youth washed Net's car while we ate our simple pide. Then we pushed on towards Izmir via Kusadasi. As we came closer to the coast the topo-graphy changed from wide-open spaces to hills covered in conifers. It felt strange to have come from the startlingly bare landscape of Cappadocia to these alpine-like slopes. When we reached the coast we could not resist a paddle in the Aegean, so at least we could say we'd done it. After nearly a day's travel-ling it was soothing to stand knee deep, trousers rolled up, in the gently lapping water.

Arriving in Izmir, we contacted Craig, who was pleased to hear the journey to Nizip had gone so well. Halit had reported back on our excursion and Craig suggested we have dinner with Halit's boss, Yomi, the following night. Yomi had made some plans for us to visit the ancient city of Ephesus (or Efes as the Turkish call it) in the morning. It is best to go there in the early part of the day before the sun, blazing down on all the white marble, makes it uncomfortably hot.

Net collected us in the morning, going first to see the Meryemana, a house where St John is believed to have brought Mary to hide after the Crucifixion. What a journey that must have been to this remote hilltop about 5 kilometres from Efes. You can see what a secure retreat it might have been, surrounded by pines and lush vegetation; the environment is probably not too different now from how it was two thousand years ago. We left the car at the top gate of Efes so we could walk downhill through the city. Net arranged for one of his mates to drive him back up to fetch it later. Built two millennia ago, Ephesus was one of the most important cities in the Roman Empire, with a population of 250,000. Now it must be one of the most awe-inspiring archaeological sites in the world. The vast plain spread out below the city was once sea before it silted up and pushed the ocean out for 10 kilometres. Antony and Cleopatra had sailed on this ocean on a state visit to this coastal gateway to the Eastern world. Its streets were paved with marble blocks, many over a metre long and just under a metre wide. Before excavation began in the nineteenth century the whole place lay buried beneath tonnes of earth and weeds. As you walk down the majestic Arcadian Street you can see where half a building has been unearthed and the remainder simply disappears, blending into the surrounding hills.

Ephesus had well-engineered drainage systems and even latrines with constantly flowing water to flush the effluent away. A popular attraction, the latrines were constructed of marble benches with holes in them about a metre apart. Apparently well-to-do gentlemen would send their personal slaves down before morning ablutions, to sit on the marble and warm it up for them. (I suspect this bit of history, and the saucy details of the brothel, are more the product of a guide's fertile imagination than some documented musings from an ancient scribe.) One cannot help but be drawn to the great Library of Celsus, an incredible façade of intricate carvings, almost entirely reconstructed by Viennese archaeologists. Near the library was a beautiful mosaic pathway over 3 metres wide. The blue and red tiles look as lovely now as they must have done when they were first laid.

We rambled through the 24,000-seat open-air theatre in the intense heat of the late morning, imagining what a spectacle the festival of Artemis must have been when celebrated by the Ephesians in this magnificent amphitheatre with its remarkable acoustics. The power of a place such as this makes one feel at peace, in awe, insignificant and humble, all at once.

We headed off and the afternoon was spent over a simple lunch of pide made by women swathed in headscarves in the pretty village of Şirince, famous for its painstakingly produced embroidery. We wandered through the cobbled streets and admired the weathered wooden shutters on the houses, held together by rusty, hand-forged nails and hiding delicate lace curtains inside. We loved the way a group of three or more windows would have lace curtains, all of different designs.

Back in Izmir that night we met up with Craig and Yomi. Yomi is a Jewish trader who deals with the herb and spice growers, and has drying and cleaning facilities of his own that he would show us the following day. Yomi charmed Liz. He is elegant, fluent in English and French and has a successful business in spite of the current inflation rate in Turkey of 100 per cent. Yomi was telling us the official inflation rate is 80 per cent and interest on loans in US dollars 25 per cent. A lot, yes, but not as much as the interest rates on local currency, which can be anything from 100 per cent to 150 per cent! We might complain about our economy sometimes, but we are fortunate not to have to cope with factors like this, which actually worsened after the Istanbul earthquake and September 11.

We walked a few blocks from the hotel to an old street that had escaped the disastrous fires that razed most of the wooden buildings in Izmir in 1924. Charming balconies and vine-covered trellises lined each side of the street, and at night the cobbled roadway was closed to traffic and filled with tables and chairs from the street-front restaurants. Yomi and Craig suggested the fish baked in salt, an impressive dish because the salt sets hard like a shell during baking. With much theatrical fanfare, the waiter brought the whole encrusted fish to the table and like a mason breaking stones in Efes, bashed it, breaking the salt crust away and sending shards of salt and brittle fins flying across the table and onto the cobbles. What was revealed was a beautifully cooked, delicate fish seasoned only with lemon juice and freshly ground black pepper. We washed the fish down with a Turkish red wine which was light and dry and perfect with the meal.

I was overwhelmed by our host's hospitality. Craig and I had exchanged numerous emails while planning the trip, Yomi had flown Halit to Gaziantep to meet us and show us the sumac, and the next day Yomi was going to take us to see his herb cleaning and processing facilities.

Over dinner I asked Craig if he knew anything about mastic, to which he replied, 'The Mastic Information Bureau has an office just one block down the road from your hotel. Why don't you go there tomorrow morning before we go on the factory tour?'

Mastic had fascinated me for some time. It is the sap from the gum mastic tree, or *schinos* as it is called on its native Greek island of Chios, not far from Izmir. A slow-growing, hardy evergreen it reaches 3 metres or more in height. The sappy gum hardens after tapping, which is referred to as 'hurting', and is seen in pieces referred to as tears. The texture of these tears is brittle and somewhat crystalline. The flavour is initially bitter and mineral-like, becoming more neutral after a few minutes chewing, when it takes on the consistency and opaque fawn colour of chewing gum.

Most of the world's production of gum mastic comes from Chios, where an unsurpassed passion and dedication to the gum mastic tree is evident, and hence the Gum Mastic Growers' Association. Mastic has a long history dating back to classical times, and is mentioned by Greek authors such as Pliny, Dioscorides, Galenus and Theophrastus. One legend, which I feel is particularly appropriate, has it that St Issidoros was tortured to death by the Romans in AD 250 and his body was dragged under the mastic tree. Upon seeing the saint's mutilated form, the tree started to cry with real tears, which appeared ever after as 'tears' of mastic. Mastic was well known to the Pharaohs, and was mentioned by Hippocrates, the ancient doctor known as 'The Father of Medicine', as a cure for all manner of ailments from baldness to intestinal and bladder problems, as a paste for toothache and to apply in cases of snakebite.

From the tenth century on, Chios became famous for its *masticha*. The name derives from the Greek word *mastichon*, which means 'to chew' and is the root of the English word masticate, for it was as a chewing gum and mouth freshener that mastic was commonly used. From the fourteenth and fifteenth centuries, the production of mastic was highly organised and controlled by the *Scriba Masticis*, clerks whose job was the registration of the production of gum mastic. As with most valuable commodities, the penalties for stealing gum mastic were draconian to say the least, and the severity related directly to the quantity stolen. Receivers of stolen mastic also had the same punishment meted out to them. These punitive measures ranged from having one's ears and/or nose cut off, to branding with red-hot steel on the forehead, or getting your eyes burnt out, to the ultimate penalty of hanging, if caught with over 200 kilograms.

The next morning, after a light breakfast including *simit* (a round bread roll shaped like a deck quoit and encrusted with golden, unhulled sesame seeds), Liz and I walked to the offices of the Mastic Information Bureau. There we met Mr Cemil Bulent Çinar, a pleasant guy who spoke English. He runs a shop on the ground floor with his brother, selling homewares and bric-a-brac, and up a narrow spiral staircase has a tiny office that is the Mastic Information Bureau. Sadly we did not have time to arrange a visit to Chios but Mr Çinar was able to give us a lot of useful advice and a comprehensive information booklet printed by the growers' association he represents. Today, the Gum Mastic Growers' Association lists sixty-four uses for mastic, extolling among other things its anti-cancer properties, use in treatment of duodenal ulcers, benefits for oral hygiene and use in South Morocco and Mauritania as an aphro-disiac! We left with samples of mastic chewing gum and a little bottle of mastic oil, which is used in making varnish for musi-cal instruments.

We were feeling quite elated – not only had we found out all about sumac, but we also had a wealth of useful infor-mation about mastic. Net was a little crestfallen when we told him we were meeting Craig and Yomi and would not need him until 3.00 pm. He loved being in the thick of it, especially when we were talking about business and the ins and outs of the spice trade. He had known little about our industry a few days ago, but I am sure from now on his tourists will be most impressed with yet another plank in his already considerable platform of knowledge.

Our first destination was Yomi's herb-cleaning plant on the other side of Izmir. Funny thing is that it is always referred to as 'the other side' even when you're there. 'Where are you?' says the incoming voice on the mobile phone. 'At the other side,' you say, even if the person calling you is next door. Yomi's car had a flat tyre so we went without him by taxi to the factory and met up again with Halit, whom we had last seen in Gaziantep. Halit phoned Net and told him of our predicament and Net, delighted that he was needed, was there by the time we finished the factory tour. The factory was as well set up as any I have seen with mostly cleaning equipment, made up of vibratory screens, de-stoning and winnowing machines.

Many people think growing and selling herbs is no more complicated than picking up grass clippings. The herbs that Yomi buys from growers (thyme, oregano, sage, spearmint and bay leaves to mention a few) are all grown on relatively small holdings. Many crops are not even in orderly cultivation, and may be gathered from plants growing wild on the hills. This material has to be cleaned to remove twigs and other contaminants. The dried leaves have to be tested for volatile oil content to meet a standard expectation of flavour, and the moisture content must be low enough to prevent the herbs from going mouldy.

Although they are not herbs and spices, Craig thought we would be interested to see the facility where Yomi produces sun-dried tomatoes, eggplant and capsicum. We went a bit more off the beaten track here, bumping along a dusty, unsealed road with caper bushes (*Capparis spinosa*) growing like weeds along the roadside. The name 'caper' is derived from the Greek word for 'he-goat' in reference to the billygoat-like aroma the pickled flower buds develop. Yomi explained how harvesting caper buds at the optimum time is as much an art as a science. Apparently buds that are just the right size are gathered in the early morning before they open with the rising sun, and then put aside to wilt for a day. These wilted buds, generally with a few millimetres of stem kept on, are put into barrels of heavily salted wine vinegar and left to pickle. During this process, capric acid develops and it is the subtle amount of acid that gives pickled capers their characteristic flavour. One wonders how anyone thought of pickling the unpleasant-tasting buds from this spiky, bramble-like bush, to produce a condiment that is a natural partner for smoked salmon. I have noticed capers produced by another process called 'dry-salting', but the result is considered inferior to the pickling method and dry-salted capers are usually cheaper in the marketplace. If the flowers are left to mature they form oval-shaped fruits which are referred to as caper berries. Sometimes these berries and even the leaves and spikes are pickled, especially in Cyprus where capers grow in alarming abundance.

The tomato processing was fascinating to watch. After being washed and halved the tomatoes were laid out on about half a hectare of woven polypropylene matting to dry in the sun. The sun-dried tomatoes made a brilliant red spectacle in the sunshine and the completely dried ones we sampled were mouthwateringly delicious. The tour complete, we sat and exchanged pleasantries with our hosts while sipping apple tea. Net drove us back from 'the other side' and for lunch we bought *simit* from a street vendor, who sold the golden, giant doughnut look-alikes from a glass-encased barrow. We decided to add golden unhulled sesame seeds to our range when we got home, even if we don't master the art of making *simit*.

Net escorted us right up to our departure gate at the airport and we bade farewell to our avuncular guide whom we really felt we had got to know over the past week. We were thankful that he was still in Izmir when the devastating earthquake hit Istanbul a week later.

The SPICES of ZANZIBAR

Who would have thought that such a common spice could cause so much angst? The turn of the century was upon us and our little spice shop had been open for two and half years. We had sourced spices from around the globe, from the mundane to the exotic, and yet in all the time I had been involved in the spice trade, I had never had so many quality issues as the ones I was now experiencing with cloves (*Eugenia caryophyllata*).

Cloves are the dried flower buds from a tropical ever-green tree that is native to the eastern Indonesian islands referred to as the Moluccas, which include Ternate, Tidor, Motir, Makian and Batjan. These buds form in clusters of ten to fifteen, and are joined together by a short length of stem, which is about the same length as a clove and is naturally enough referred to as a 'clove stem'. The best cloves are handpicked when they have reached full size, and although still predominantly green, they will be streaked with flashes of bright pink, reminding one of the unopened eyes of baby marsupials.

If the buds are not gathered, they will flower and turn into oblong, drooping fruits known as 'mother of cloves' which, although they sound wonderful, have no use in the spice trade. As with many spices, when the cloves are put out in the sun to dry, the enzymic reaction creates the flavour. It turns the cloves a reddish brown to dark brown and forms a volatile oil called eugenol. Dried cloves are approximately 10 to 15 millimetres long, and are nail-shaped and tapered at one end. Interestingly the name 'clove' derives from the Latin *clavus* meaning 'nail'; their name in German is *Nelken* which means 'little nails', and the Chinese *ting hiang* means 'nail spice'. The bud end has a friable, paler ball appearing to sit atop four engagement-ring-style clasps and good quality, handpicked cloves will still have this ball intact.

The cause of my concern was the large quantity of clove stems that were in so many batches of cloves sent to me. Clove stems look very similar to cloves, except that they are like a little straight stick instead of a nail-shaped clove. The main problem is that clove stems have only about 15 per cent of the volatile oil that is found in cloves. So while commercially it may be okay to use these stems to make clove-stem oil, a popular ingredient in the beverage and confectionery industries, it is totally unacceptable to have clove stems in a retail pack of cloves. By the time we had picked out the stems, some batches were yielding only just over half the original weight.

So why the apparent decline in standards? Much of the reason was attributed to the drop in the world supply of cloves, which was partly due to fires in Indonesia that had damaged some plantations, and because the islands of Madagascar and Zanzibar, off the east coast of Africa, were not producing cloves to their usual standards. When the price of cloves starts to increase and supply becomes scarcer, we always notice more incidents of adulteration, either through laziness or design, with higher amounts of clove stems among the cloves.

We had seen cloves being harvested and dried in India, and although many cloves are grown in India, it is usually Indonesian cloves that are imported into Australia as it is so close. Indonesia consumes a large quantity of cloves in the manufacture of *kretek* cigarettes, those distinctive aromatic ones that crackle as they burn. When I smell a *kretek* cigarette, no matter what country I am in, it immediately transports me back to Asia.

Liz and I decided that we should learn still more about the harvesting and trading of cloves, and hopefully find a top quality supplier who could guarantee premium-grade, hand-picked cloves without stems. For this exercise we nominated Zanzibar, a country which had only been growing cloves since the late eighteenth century, but by the late nineteenth century was supplying close to 90 per cent of the world's clove trade. It seemed logical to visit the place that had once been such an important producer and to understand why its market dominance of the trade had diminished.

Zanzibar is one of those place names that conjure up exotic images. Its zeds put your tongue between your teeth, while the mere act of pronunciation makes the mouth fizz, as if you'd just tasted a tangy spice. Having had no previous trading connections with Zanzibar, I knew I would have to start from square one. I also found that all correspondence stopped abruptly as soon as I made mention of talking to growers or visiting farms. I think the old suspicions aroused by another trader trying to find out just a little bit too much were the reasons for the walls of silence. We made plans to go there anyway and conduct our own investigations. This was our first trip to Africa and the excitement of heading off to a new destination filled our waking moments as we finalised our travel plans.

The main island of Zanzibar is called Unguja, is only about 80 kilometres long and has an area of about 1500 square kilometres. Pemba, the next largest island in the group, just north of Unguja, is roughly half that size. Situated 40 kilometres off the east coast of Africa, it is most readily accessed from the Tanzanian capital Dar es Salaam. Further east lies the Indian Ocean Comoros group of islands and Madagascar to the south of those. On the mainland to the north of Tanzania is Somalia, which the Egyptians voyaged to in 1500 BC when it was known as 'The Land of Punt'. Part of the rich history of this part of the world was the attraction for Arab traders of finding precious metals, ivory, exotic animals and spices.

Landing in Dar es Salaam, we soon realised that this was not the place to be if you were in a hurry and we'd better get into *mañana* mode pretty quickly if the blood pressure was to be kept under control. It took over an hour just to queue for our visas and change some currency into Tanzanian shillings (about 600 shillings to the Australian dollar). The taxi was an old Corolla that would have looked more at home in a wrecker's yard. Bits of crisp and curling torn vinyl were poking out everywhere, the lining was missing from one back door, window winders were missing or swinging useless and pendulum-like as we bumped along the road. Most of the traffic and street lights didn't seem to be working, and when the driver did get to a red light, he drove straight through. In the dark, Dar es Salaam felt spooky, lacking the familiar hubbub and population density of cities in India. As the taxi sped as best it could, smelling of petrol and burning oil, away from the CBD and into pitch darkness, Liz and I looked at each other with just a modicum of alarm. We knew the resort we were booked into was a way out of town, and who knew what we'd encounter on the way.

After another half hour of driving we finally pulled up at a dimly lit, doubtful-looking establishment which didn't appear as though it was worth US$120 a night. It was midnight and the only person on duty was a huge unsmiling Tanzanian who checked us in. He showed us to our room, past a Mexican-inspired restaurant with poky booth tables and an aroma of rodents, through a half-finished construction zone glowing in the moonlight, down a little dingy hall and finally into our room. Our first impression was that we might have found a hotel that would surpass the 'end of the world' special in Bombay. However, after the initial shock of wild-west decor, complete with six framed pictures of cowboys in sombreros, and Mexican wall hangings, we thought that it might be all right after all.

I had made contact with a few traders in Dar es Salaam before leaving Australia and had planned to spend two days here before getting the ferry to Zanzibar. Phone calls to all but one proved pointless. The chap I spoke to gave us the name of his spice-farming relative in Zanzibar, a Mr Kissassi who apparently owned the Jumbo Guest House, and would be easy to find once we got there.

Oyster Bay beckoned and we thought we had better have a good look at it before doing anything else. The position of the hotel was quite splendid, across the road from the bay, a sweep of beach about a kilometre long. There were signs in the hotel warning patrons not to take money or wear jewellery, not even watches, or wander too far from the immediate vicinity because a number of people had been robbed, some violently. Before leaving the hotel the receptionist told us to stay near the Masai guard on the beach and to ask him to watch us if we walked a little way from the hotel. Masai men seem to have a reputation as security guards here and this man looked quite splendid with his bright red robes, long, plaited hair and fierce spear. He was even standing with one foot resting against the inside of his knee, like the subject of a Victorian painting. The whole ensemble was beautifully set off by his incongruous pair of white plastic sandals. Nonetheless, these tall, graceful, taciturn bodyguards are the kind of guys you wouldn't say boo to and he certainly made us feel a little more secure.

The tide was out in Oyster Bay, and rather than looking at an Indian Ocean resort beach of natural splendour, the sands were coated with a film of mud and debris left by the high tide, featuring many cigarette packets and plastic bags.

Back safely in the hotel, we spent another couple of hours trying to get to see someone in the spice trade in Dar es Salaam, however when this looked hopeless, we brought our plans forward and decided to take a ferry to Zanzibar after lunch, hot-footing it out of there as quickly as possible.

When the taxi pulled up at the wharf we felt like a couple of fresh cow-pats with a load of flies descending upon them. We were surrounded by a mass of faces, with everyone talking at once and hoping to relieve us of our money in exchange for the provision of some unmentionable goods or dodgy service.

The taxi driver was very good and stayed with us while we bought our ferry tickets and a porter was arranged to carry our bags. The hour-long wait for the ferry passed quickly enough as we watched the constant stream of humanity moving to and fro with all manner of merchandise and worldly goods. Some were carrying huge, rough-sawn planks that I would have had trouble moving, let alone carrying. Others had equally weighty baskets of pineapples, boxes of books, cartons of eggs and clothes that were tied up in enormous bales.

The seashore around the dock was littered with rotting and rusting hulks, the skeletal remains beached or half-submerged where they had completed their last voyage. It was an incongruous scene of desolation and hopelessness set against a most beautiful stretch of ocean.

The crowd began to stir; something was obviously afoot. Large women in brightly coloured clothes carrying bundles wrapped in printed cloth and appearing to be carrying more children than they had arms to hold were jostling towards the waterfront. The Zanzibar ferry docked and a sea of people swarmed past us up the gangplank, colliding, tangling and meshing with the tidal wave of people clambering to get off the vessel. Our porter carried our bags to the diesel-fuming ferry and we followed him through the dilapidated second-class deck, up clattering steel steps and into the plush but soiled first-class area.

The ferry arrived at 3.30 pm and hovered for thirty minutes before gliding into the dock. We are still not too sure of the reason for the wait; perhaps it was to allow us to take in the sight of Zanzibar, with its picturesque buildings lining the waterfront. The sun shining behind us, we gazed across turquoise water to the stone-coloured houses, hotels, offices and warehouses; the place we would call home for the next week.

The Hotel Tembo (*tembo* means elephant in Swahili) is a charming building with Portuguese and Arab influences. The façade is whitewashed and studded with heavy-framed, dark wooden windows and shutters. Our room was on the second floor and looked onto a swimming pool in the courtyard and out to the beach and Prison Island just offshore. The room felt positively antique with its high double bed, the ornate bed-heads works of art in themselves. Painted tiles, mirrors and coloured glass were set into the timber, creating an image of an elaborate resting galleon set off by sails of fine mosquito nets. A bed more than adequate for a spice merchant to recline upon!

We thought we would have no trouble spending a week here and went out for a stroll through the Stone Town streets behind the hotel. We found them as captivating as Istanbul, Mattancherry, Colombo or Kumily. Narrow streets and over-hanging verandahs created an optical illusion of two- and three-storey houses leaning towards each other, as if neighbours on either side could reach out and shake hands. Although the Muslim-owned Hotel Tembo is dry, and alcohol is not even permitted in the rooms, there are bars where one can down a couple of cool Tusker beers and watch the dhows silhouetted against the coppery setting sun.

We were in the mood for local fare for dinner and Liz had pilau rice with beef that was quite tasteless considering we were on one of the world's most fabled spice islands. The beef was within a whisker of becoming biltong and my fish with green bananas was only marginally tastier. I thought it was interesting how like potatoes the green bananas were when cooked, and that just a little bit of cumin, garam masala or chilli would have made all the difference.

Markets in most countries are an excellent noisy barometer of what the locals buy to eat and how they go about their daily lives, so that's where we headed the next day. On the way we came across a little noodle-making factory. The noodles were neatly laid out to dry in hundreds of woollen-skein-sized tangles that looked more like a haberdashery stall from a distance than a noodle business. The air grew heavy with the smell of dried fish and we suspected we were heading in the right direction. As if to confirm that our radar was in working order, the spice sellers were the first section we came to.

Our enthusiasm and interest made stall holders immediately suspicious of our motives, and it was only after we had exchanged a few 'in' comments, the spice merchant's equivalent to the Masonic handshake, nod, wink, or secret password, that they loosened up. Their cardamom pods were straw coloured and although reasonably tasty, lacked the fresh, aromatic topnotes of the peacock-green Guatemalan and South Indian cardamom. The reason for this was that they had been dried in the sun and, unlike many spices that benefit from the sun's intense heat to develop their flavours, with cardamom it only serves to bleach out both colour and complexity of taste.

Their cinnamon was true cinnamon (*Cinnamomum zeylanicum*) not cassia (*C. cassia*) but the pieces were thick chips of complete bark instead of the separated underneath layer as we saw in Sri Lanka. This grade is very similar to what we often call Seychelles cinnamon; it has the true mild flavour of good cinnamon although the sweetness and aromatic, almost lemony-fresh notes are not there. What we really did appreciate, though, were the whole nutmegs on sale still in their shell and with their deep red *aril* of mace clinging on, intact. I was interested to see how red the dried mace was compared to mace I have seen in other countries. Either the drying is done very carefully, difficult to believe when you look at the cardamoms, or it has something to do with when the fruits are harvested. We bought several packets of nutmegs and a delightful wreath about as thick as my wrist, made entirely from cloves strung and bound together.

There were fruits and vegetables laid out in typical marketplace profusion. Liz found the fresh meat section somewhat stomach-churning as we walked through what amounted to an on-the-spot abattoir. The whole fresh bullock's head staring at us from a bloody shelf above rows of calves' feet with the skin and hair on, drove us to move on and we strode briskly towards the old slave market for more disturbing sights.

In 1772 slavery was declared illegal in England. By 1807 the British Empire abolished slave trading, and the United States followed in 1808. Over the next few years the French and the Germans also passed laws against the slave trade. Zanzibar was an entrepôt in this cruel trade. Our visit to the slave market cells, where thirty to forty slaves had been crammed in, shackled and waiting to be sold, was moving and disturbing. About 8000 slaves a year were brought over from the African mainland to Zanzibar, along with shipments of ivory.

With the abolition of slavery gaining momentum, Zanzibar had a surplus of slaves, until an Arab by the name of Saleh bin Haramil al Abray established clove plantations where the slaves were put to work. Cloves had been a valuable commodity for over three centuries and were one of the major spices, along with nutmeg, that fostered the spice trade and remarkable voyages of discovery in the sixteenth and seventeenth centuries. The catch was that cloves only grew on the handful of tiny islands in the Indonesian archipelago mentioned earlier. From 1514 the Portuguese controlled the clove trade and the search for spices in general was on in earnest. In 1522, the only surviving ship of Magellan's circumnavigation fleet returned to Spain with 26 tonnes of cloves, more than enough to cover the entire cost of the expedition. The captain, Sebastian del Cano, was rewarded with a pension and a coat of arms comprising three nutmegs, two sticks of cinnamon and twelve cloves.

The Portuguese monopoly in the Moluccas was broken by the Dutch, who expelled them in 1605 and ruthlessly maintained control using cruel and gruesome measures for another 200 years. Part of the Dutch strategy to keep the high prices for cloves was to restrict by law the cultivation of cloves to the island of Amboina, now known as Ambon, and uproot and burn clove trees growing on other islands. The death penalty was imposed on anyone cultivating or selling cloves anywhere except Amboina. Nonetheless, numerous attempts were made from 1750 to the early 1800s to break this stranglehold on the clove trade.

What was not lost on Saleh bin Haramil al Abray was the successful breaking of the Dutch monopoly on the clove trade by the superintendent of Ile de France (now known as Mauritius). The intrepid Frenchman named Pierre Poivre (the original Peter Piper of the nursery rhyme), smuggled some 'mother of cloves' out of Amboina and propagated a small number of trees. With varying degrees of success clove plantations were established on Reunion, Martinique, Haiti and in the Seychelles. By the early nineteenth century cloves had been established on Zanzibar.

Sultan Said of Oman was like an absentee landlord and ruled his kingdom, which included Zanzibar, from Muscat. In 1827 he sailed to Zanzibar and made a commercial treaty with America, mostly involving the trade in ivory. He soon realised, though, that to grow Zanzibar's wealth he would have to increase trade with America and Europe and he identified the clove trade as a means to achieve his objectives. The ill-fated Saleh bin Haramil al Abray had all his plantations confiscated because Sultan Said saw him as a political threat. Sultan Said then decreed that three clove trees should be planted for every coconut palm on Zanzibar and Pemba, making Zanzibar one of the world's largest producers by the time he died in 1856.

Stone Town is the oldest part of the township of Zanzibar. It is quite small, like a miniature city, and the streets are all so close together they make it seem even more compact. Instead of a block as we know it of buildings between streets, Stone Town is a maze of alleys, not much more than 2 metres wide and generally only one building apart.

Wandering through these alleys, we would pass indolent, rheumy-eyed men lolling on their doorsteps in front of ornate doors. Friendly young men would greet us with '*Jambo*' (hello), and not so genuine touts would accost us with the hope of selling some of the dusty, feeble merchandise on display in the dark room behind them, or offer to arrange 'Spice Tour for sir and madam, Prison Island Tour, swim with dolphins, you want taxi, sir, change money – US dollar?' And so it would go on as we continued exploring Stone Town.

I loved the buildings, flanking shady alleys with distorted, bulging walls that lean more than 10 degrees from the perpendicular. They look as though the ingress of moisture, the ravages of time and subsequent softening of their basic mud and coral building materials have organically pushed them out of shape. It is as if they are growing, changing and alive. Is it possible that these tipsy, soft-edged houses and shops looked much the same when they were built? I heard a wonderful expression recently when some friends described their slow house renovations as 'arrested decay', an excuse for never properly fixing anything. I thought that summed up what the Zanzibarians will have to do with Stone Town. It would be sad for it to decline further and even worse for it to be reconstructed and sanitised like Singapore.

For all its beauty and mystique, Stone Town does feel a bit oppressive after a couple of hours. You walk along one lane with houses almost touching above you, then what looks convincingly like a dead end morphs into an opening and reveals a narrow lane heading off into another. Hours of wandering took us in a number of circles, yet no matter how long we spent in Stone Town, or how far we seemed to strike off in a different direction, whenever we decided to head back to the seafront we would find it again in a matter of minutes. The sea breeze would lure us and as we rounded a blind corner a vista to the turquoise blue ocean would be waiting for us.

To start our search for the clove contact given to us in Dar es Salaam, we consulted the guidebook, which showed a

Jumbo Guest House not far from the markets. After a few false starts we found it, only to be told that Mr Kissassi was at a different Jumbo Guest House and it was in Kozani. We could not find Kozani on our map and wondered if it was Jozani, instead. Hot and sweaty, we tramped back to the hotel, cooled off with a swim and had for lunch a basic *thali* of lightly curried chicken, shredded cabbage with brown mustard seeds and sambar served with rice, in a little Indian restaurant around the corner. Eating here was more like being in someone's home, which it basically was. There was only one item on the menu and whatever had been prepared was served. Simple, tasty and just cooked, it started to restore our faith in Zanzibarian food.

After lunch I collared an obliging-looking taxi driver and negotiated his services for the rest of the day to help me track down the elusive Mr Kissassi and more information about the Zanzibar clove industry while Liz enjoyed relaxing by the Indian Ocean. The driver's name was Salim Bomber and he said to just call him Bom-Ber, with the accent on the second 'b'. He seemed to know where Kozani was, and after asking for directions a few times and making a couple of U-turns, we bounced off the road and down a rough, stony track in the jungle until we came to the Jumbo Guest House, which looked a little like a military camp. The uniformed guard at the gate let us through and indicated where the reception area was. Our eyes took a minute or two to adjust to the dark inside where a very old man with white whiskers was fast asleep on a couch. Bom-Ber and I woke him up and he went away mumbling something and came back with a blank-faced young woman. She escorted us to another part of the complex where I finally met Mr Kissassi. Dressed in dark trousers and a crisp white shirt, he was round-faced and jolly. I couldn't help noticing an enormous gold ring on his right-hand ring finger. It was embossed with the sails of twin dhows and looked like a company seal.

He explained that when Zanzibar achieved independence and the Marxist government seized all privately owned clove plantations and gave them to the people, the clove industry went into decline. The new owners ceased maintaining the trees as they should have and in a relatively short time Zanzibar lost its dominant position in the world market. He also explained that even small quantities of cloves would have to be bought through the State Trading Corporation and that I should be talking to them. Mr Kissassi gave detailed directions to Bom-Ber and we drove back into town to offices at the wharves.

Here we were confronted with an entrenched public service apathy. Someone eventually told us we should be talking to the head honcho in the main office, which is? You guessed it, one block from the Tembo Hotel. Bom-Ber was starting to feel quite proprietorial towards me by now and as my local associate he accompanied me to the main office, where we were systematically ushered through three stages of offices, each one neater and more important than the last. The final office was that of the Mr Salieman Jongo, Marketing Officer of the Zanzibar State Trading Corporation, the only downside being that he was away on leave. Another official did see me and he explained that last season's crop had all been sold, but was a bit vague about the ability to supply a top-notch grade completely free of stem. 'Pick 'em, dry 'em and sell 'em off as fast as we can' was the message I got loud and clear. He did at least give me a small sample of standard-grade cloves and their flavour and aroma was actually very good, except for the pieces of stem. He then wrote out a sample certificate in quadruplicate for quarantine clearance on our return to Australia.

When we left the office, Bom-Ber informed me that Mr Jongo is a relative (everyone in Zanzibar seems to be related) and he would try to arrange a meeting at Mr Jongo's home in a couple of days. So the saga continues . . . Needless to say we never met and two years later, every time I send a fax or letter to coincide with the clove harvest between July and January — deafening silence.

It seemed unlikely that we were going to be able to dig any deeper through trade channels, so Liz and I decided to go on a spice tour. Fisherman Tours, the company we had booked our accommodation through over the internet, arranged for a fellow by the name of Jackson to drive us north of Zanzibar town towards Bububu and then inland to a government-owned spice garden. As soon as we arrived I noticed a head-high plant that looked like a weed. It was covered in four-chambered seed capsules, each 2 centimetres long. It was in fact sesame (*Sesamum indicum*) and it was pleasing to find it here, as it is native to tropical Africa.

Sesame is possibly the oldest crop that was grown for edible oil and there are many ancient records of its use. A 4000-year-old drawing on an Egyptian tomb depicts a baker adding sesame seeds to dough, and the remains of sesame seeds were found in a chamber of the excavated ruins of the Old Testament kingdom of Ararat. In the tale 'Ali Baba and the Forty Thieves', the magic password was 'Open sesame', an appropriate phrase as a fully ripe sesame pod dramatically shatters open at the slightest touch. The use of sesame became widespread in Africa and in the seventeenth and eighteenth centuries African slaves, many of whom were traded through Zanzibar, took sesame to America. Our guide was interested to hear that *benne*, their name for it, still means sesame in parts of America's south. Unfortunately the seed capsules on these plants were not ripe enough for me to try the 'open sesame' trick.

When we were shown plots of cardamom, I commented that they would fetch a much better price for the cardamom if it was not dried in the sun. But I think the alternative sounded like too much trouble. I spotted another variety of cardamom plant with spherical yellow-orange pods borne on stems from the centre. This made me very excited, as I thought it might have been 'grains of paradise', also known as melegueta pepper (*Aframomum amomum*). Grains of paradise are the peppery, camphor-like seeds from a member of the cardamom family that is indigenous to the West Coast of Africa. The herbalist John Gerard mentions the medicinal virtues of grains of paradise and both the seeds and rhizomes were known to be used medicinally in West Africa. The seeds were not as pungent as they should be, however green cardamom seeds are not very strong until dried either. I suspect this plant may have been a type of melegueta pepper, but as I would not have been able to bring fresh seeds back into Australia to dry and positively identify, it remains one of life's little mysteries.

We also saw annatto (*Bixa orellana*) trees, with heart-shaped, glossy leaves providing an attractive background to large, bright pink flowers that have the appearance of wild roses. After flowering, prickly, heart-shaped, scarlet seed pods form. They look uncannily like Oscar the Grouch. No wonder it is also called the lipstick tree because just a smear of the bright-red pulp surrounding the seeds is as effective as many commercial lipsticks. We were shown nutmeg drying with the mace intact, and after much discussion concluded that their very red mace may have something to do with the fact that the nutmeg fruits are almost overripe when harvested.

There was an abundant crop of bird's eye chillies, the local name for them being *piri piri ho ho*. *Piri piri*, *peri peri* and *pilli pilli* are names commonly used in Africa to describe chillies, the *ho ho* suffix simply means 'very hot', which these minute chillies are. A fairly straggly collection of pepper vines, some clove trees and various citrus and other fruit trees filled up the rest of the spice garden. We were pleased we'd taken the tour.

Back in town we dined at the night markets in a waterfront park called Forodhani Gardens. After our first couple of nights we thought we should risk taking some local street food, and we were drawn to the charcoal-fragrant, smoke-hazed cooking aromas. Under the light of hurricane lanterns and on makeshift stalls, the vendors were selling varieties of fish, octopus, crab and prawns, strung onto skewers and barbecued. At the stall that interested us most a man was making *pisa*. He placed a circle of stretched dough about 20 centimetres in diameter on a hotplate and then put spoonfuls of ingredients on top of it – cooked mince, shredded onion and capsicum, some chilli sauce and optional slices of *piri piri ho ho*. He then broke an egg over the lot and daddled it around with a spoon until it was a homogeneous slurry, before folding the edges of the circle back in to make a neat parcel. When it was cooked and firm he presented the pisa to us on a paper plate. Delicious.

We spent a few more days doing touristy things and in

no time it was the day of our departure. Instead of booking the ferry back we decided to lash out and splurge on taking the hydrofoil to Dar es Salaam. We would be flying from Dar to Johannesburg and then on to Australia, and didn't want to risk missing our connections. Over the last week of our stay we had seen a number of plush craft plying the Indian Ocean waters between Zanzibar and Dar and wondered which one of these might be our transport. The hydrofoil that arrived looked like something out of Jules Verne's *Forty Thousand Leagues Under the Sea*. It was sleek, angled and marlin-like, but it had the appearance of a futuristic impression of a hydrofoil drawn in 1890. The hull was rippled with numerous dents, and another corker was added to its nose when it was berthed at our jetty. Liz exclaimed as it crashed into the pontoon, 'I hope he hasn't made a hole in it.' To which an American couple who had inspected the damage pronounced, 'It's okay, the hole is above the waterline.'

The trip to Dar es Salaam was smoother than expected and as we flew from Dar to Jo'burg we thought that our next trip should reacquaint us with Asia. Most of my activities in and around Singapore were related to trading and processing, and although not as structured as India's spice trade, huge quantities of spices are grown in that region. As fate would have it, our desire to find out more about a spice that causes a great deal of confusion took us to a remote village in North Vietnam.

BARKING UP
the WRONG TREE

When we opened our spice shop we were surprised by the number of customers who had comments, both positive and negative, about the various grades of cinnamon they had been buying over the years. A quick sniff of a tester jar of ground cinnamon quills followed by a comforting inhalation of ground cassia soon solved any apprehension about which type of cinnamon they were looking for.

We found that there was confusion between cinnamon and cassia, something that has dogged growers and traders, processors and consumers. One of the world's most popular and well-known spices, cinnamon can easily be confused with cassia – a spice that is just as popular. True cinnamon, as we discovered on 'Stanley's Farm', is native to Sri Lanka and is the underneath layer of bark from the tree *Cinnamomum zeylanicum*.

There is another cinnamon, which originates in Asia,

that is arguably used by more than half the world's population. This so-called Asian cinnamon is actually cassia and comes from a related tree, *Cinnamomum cassia*. Cassia has a stronger, more perfumed aroma than cinnamon and the flavour bears an agreeable sharpness and hot aftertaste. Ground cassia is slightly darker and more reddish brown than ground cinnamon.

Cassia is very popular in the United States and for many years was sold as a premium-grade product under the name of Saigon Cinnamon. Now it has become the standard and is just referred to there as cinnamon. To add to our confusion in Australia, the old Pure Food Act in New South Wales made it illegal to sell cassia as cinnamon. This law was probably initiated because cassia was considerably cheaper than cinnamon and the lawmakers in their wisdom thought its use as an inferior substitute should be stamped out. These days it is simply called cinnamon, baker's cinnamon or Dutch cinnamon.

One can easily distinguish whole cinnamon from whole cassia, because when viewed in cross section, cinnamon quills are composed of many concentric layers of very thin bark, no more than a millimetre thick – the spice equivalent to a Flake chocolate bar. Cassia, on the other hand, will be seen in either large flat pieces, 5 to 20 centimetres long, or in quills of thick bark scrolled in a single layer. I like to chew on a little cassia bark, its mouth-freshening sweetness and slightly medicinal, warm flavour tastes far more agreeable and natural than American cinnamon chewing gum which is actually flavoured with oil extracted from cassia or artificial flavours.

The best cassia in the world is reputed to come from Vietnam, although it is also grown in large quantities in China and Indonesia. Because I have seen so many grades of cassia in the trade I thought it was about time Liz and I went to the country that has the best reputation for cassia production. Then we could see for ourselves where it grows and how it is harvested and processed. I was also interested in visiting that part of the world I had read about when researching the history of the spice trade, Cochin China, as South Vietnam was known in the seventeenth century.

No sooner had we made the decision to go to Vietnam than I came across an article on the internet about an American cinnamon trader who was in a joint-venture with the Vietnamese government. The article was about Mark Barnett and his company Pacific Basin Partnership, which exports premium-grade cassia to major world markets. From the first email contact I knew we would get along. Mark's family had owned a small spice company in the USA and very much like my family's small herb and spice business, it had been smothered by the giant companies in the trade. The other thing we had in common was that we had both directed our expertise to specialty segments of the market. I told Mark that my business was very small and I would probably not be a significant buyer, to which he replied, 'It will be pleasure enough to help a fellow spice brother.'

So with just a touch of trepidation we booked our flights to Hanoi.

When I was managing the spice company in Singapore, I travelled to Indonesia, Malaysia, Thailand, the Philippines, and Hong Kong and had also been to Korea and Japan. But I'd never made it to Vietnam; perhaps subconsciously it was 'off limits'. I was a teenager in the 1960s, missed the draft and became painfully aware of those unlucky enough to have their number come up and be drafted into a war that to this day sits uneasily in our national psyche. Would a pair of Australians from a former enemy nation be welcome? We'd been warned about officialdom and the need to ensure that every item of documentation was absolutely correct. We copied everything to be on the safe side – passports, visas, tickets, credit cards, traveller's cheques, itinerary and accommodation vouchers.

So in January 2002, after a three-hour flight from Singapore, we landed. Hanoi was surrounded by a dim haze, a combination of damp air blowing down from southern China and large-city pollution. It took us an hour to get through immigration. There were no problems, just pleasant khaki and red epauletted officials who read, checked and re-read every word we'd written on the entrance paper and checked it against the passport and visa. An official airport taxi driver approached us inside the terminal, we agreed on a price, and as he wheeled our bags out to the car I said to Liz, 'He seems to be kosher.' Overhearing me, the driver turned around and gave us big grin. Maybe he'd been exposed to Australians before.

The drive into Hanoi took about forty-five minutes and right up to the outskirts of the city it was obvious that this is an agrarian economy. There were few signs of industry, lots of rice paddies, some dotted with farmers and oxen, and ominous sections near the road with neat gatherings of white concrete graves rising out of the watery fields. War dead? We passed stands of narrow houses, terrace-style, no wider than the length of a motorbike but rising to three or more storeys high. Some stood alone with no buildings on either side, giving them a surreal and precarious appearance, as if the next puff of wind would blow them over like a house of cards. Driving into

Hanoi we saw shop-houses with iron gates, bikes with two or more family members riding pillion, balconies hanging over streets, flagging their occupants' daily washing, women carrying intolerable loads, and heard traffic horns constantly tooting. But for the faces of the people and the aromas lingering in the air, we felt we could have been in India, East Africa or Turkey.

Arriving at the hotel we checked in and headed for the markets. In the old quarter in Hoan Kiem District, streets are dedicated to specific merchandise, the range of which we had never seen before in such concentration. We explored 'hat street' where every size, shape and colour of hat was on display. Imelda Marcos would have run out of choices in 'shoe street' and the best stocked hardware store in Australia would pale to insignificance in 'electric motor street'.

A few streets away we came to 'grog corner'. At least a dozen traders, each with shopfronts no wider than a bus, formed a veritable wall of hard liquor. Every shop appeared to carry the same range and one was virtually a mirror image of the other. I thought, what a marketing challenge and a shopper's dream, to have so many shops that can only differentiate themselves from their competitors by price. Opposite 'grog corner' was 'birdcage lane', sporting a selection of wicker birdcages that would inspire almost anyone to choose a feathered friend as a pet. Liz bought a delightful birdcage when we lived in Singapore, however we could never quite bring ourselves to keep something as free and joyful as a songbird in a cage. Fearing that an empty birdcage would look a bit ridiculous, our youngest daughter Sophie bought a little blue imitation bird that we called Larry (because he never asked for food, kept his cage clean and was always 'happy as Larry' no matter what the weather). Tempted as we were to buy a new cage for Larry, we decided that it would be unwieldy to bring home.

We found one of the city's many markets set up under blue tarpaulins, spanning a narrow street and crammed with stalls. The vendors were unimpressed by our presence there. Perhaps from experience they viewed our interest in their merchandise as idle curiosity from ignorant tourists that would bring no repeat business, if any business at all. They were selling crockery, vegetables and fruit (we did buy a bag of delicious little apples about the size of small plums and with a single stone inside rather than the core of pips we are used to). Freshly butchered whole tiny chickens, handful-sized portions of thinly sliced beef and a delectable looking basket of roasted grubs were all on display. A less appetising but incredibly beautiful display was a selection of preserving jars, each about the size of a Vacola bottling jar, that contained snakes, lizards and herbs which resembled ginseng in a yellow-tinged liquor. The reptiles had been painstakingly arranged in the jars in a way that was reminiscent of the displays of preserved fruit in the district exhibits at the Royal Easter Show. One had a cobra that was holding a bright green little snake in its jaws, and in Hippocratic-symbol style, curved like an 'S' down in front of the cobra. One could only imagine the reaction from the friendly quarantine officer at the airport if you tried to bring one of those babies into the country. We asked the vendor what they were for and she replied in English, 'For arthritis and hot limbs.' I don't doubt her, but I'd opt for the arthritis and hot limbs any day.

Our market adventure nearly complete, we were a little taken aback by the prepared dog carcasses, complete with tails.

We were told later that it was bad luck to eat dog in the first half of the month (we still don't know why) and good luck to eat it in the last two weeks of a month – 'Very warming. Especially in winter when men, not ladies, have a few drinks, eat dog and come home very happy.' We wondered why it is that the thought of eating dog is so repugnant to those from Western cultures. If we eat Babe, Bambi and the Little White Bull, why not Lassie? Many Europeans eat horsemeat – perhaps if we as a nation were in hungrier circumstances, we would not be so judgemental.

We were impressed by the shop-house in Hanoi. The narrow three- and four-storey terraces featured distinctly French-inspired balconies and rooflines influenced by two centuries of French rule over this much-occupied country. Occasionally we felt like Gulliver-proportioned giants when we crouched on 30 centimetre high plastic stools to have our shoes shined or attempted conversation with a street-restaurant vendor. These entrepreneurial women position their establishments on little more than a metre of footpath, feed no more than two or three patrons at a time, and cook the most delicious-looking noodle soups. Garnishes include slices of bright red chilli and fresh tangles of aromatic herbs such as Vietnamese mint (*Polygonum odoratum*). Known in Vietnam as *rau ram*, this is not a member of the mint family at all but is a *Polygonaceae*. *Polygonum* literally means 'many kneed' and is a direct reference to the jointed, tangled and angled appearance of its stems. To avoid possible confusion with mint it is also called 'laksa leaf', the fragrant, coriander- and citrus-like aroma and taste making it a perfect accompaniment to laksa.

We made little progress with the language and decided

to postpone sampling street food until we were with a knowledgeable local. I was fascinated by the fuel blocks burning
under blackened woks and pots, and discovered later that these
10 centimetre round 'bricks', studded with finger-sized holes,
are made from coal dust and kerosene. The smoke from these
briquettes, when mingled with street-cooking smells, can be
positively appetising.

On the telephone that night Mark went to great pains to
let us know that the trip would not be comfortable and some of
it would have to be done on a motorbike. 'Are you sure Liz
wants to go?' he asked, to which I replied, 'She has been with
me off the beaten track in India, Mexico and Turkey in search
of spices, and while Provence and the Côte d'Azur may be more
to her liking, she's endured many uncomfortable rides in pursuit of yet another spice.' Duly satisfied that we were up to the
task, Mark told us that while he had work to do in Hanoi, his
wife Yen, assistants Miss Van Anh and Miss Huong and his
driver would look after us for the next two days.

The next morning Mark and the entourage picked us up
in his Mercedes minibus and we headed towards his factory in
the Gia Lam district, just out of Hanoi and surrounded by rice
paddies in what looked to us like rural tranquillity.

On the drive there, sandals kicked off and reclining in
the leather seat of his minibus, Mark explained how his grandfather, Norman Barnett, had started a spice-packing business in
New York in the 1940s. Mark, who is short, dark and very
New York in a Woody Allen sort of way, recalled how by the
mid 1990s he could not compete in supermarkets with the
giants, McCormick and Spice Islands. Oddly enough, Spice
Islands was owned by the Australian company Burns Philp,

which was to face some well-publicised financial trauma of its own. It appears the old firm's decision-makers were captivated by the spice trade and overestimated its financial rewards and underestimated its perils, as so many have in centuries past. A flurry of unwise acquisitions around the globe, weak strategies and pressure from impatient shareholders, led to a sell-off of most of Burns Philp's spice assets less than six years after they were acquired.

On a brighter note, as fortune would have it Mark was working on the export of chillies and garlic from China in 1993 when travel to Vietnam was legalised. A contact in New York suggested to Mark that he visit Hanoi and meet one of the managers of Generalexim, the Vietnam National General Export Import Corporation, Do Dinh Thi. Mark started with a small investment to establish trust and worked with Generalexim exporting pepper and cassia. He was the first person to import spices from Vietnam into the United States since the lifting of the embargo in 1994. Mark now claims to be the premier exporter of Vietnamese cassia to all world markets and is an inspiring example of what ingenuity, hard work and persistence can achieve.

The factory comprised mostly warehouses and a large concrete courtyard, which, in the harvesting seasons of March and August, is entirely covered with dark brown cassia bark. Harvesting takes place in the wet season when the bark is easiest to remove. As we were there in January, the workers were cleaning and grading stockpiled material from the previous harvest. I was interested to see how deftly the blue-uniformed, surgical-masked women were scraping the end of each 30 centimetre scroll of bark. When I asked what they were doing, Mark showed me how scraping along the cross-section reveals a narrow, dark oil-line. It is the intensity of that line that indicates the concentration of volatile oil. The best quality cassia will have around 4.5 per cent volatile oil content. This quick method of grading is an ideal way to sort the bark before a laboratory analysis is conducted. In another area, workers were scraping and cleaning the graded cassia bark prior to breaking it into 10 to 20 centimetre slivers ready for bagging and shipping. Most of Mark's cassia is exported in this form, and then ground in the country it is shipped to. If the cassia is ground in Vietnam and then has a two-month sea journey, the volatile oils will evaporate to such an extent that the quality will drop noticeably.

For a foreigner to operate a business in Vietnam it is necessary to be in a joint-venture with a state corporation, and in Mark's case his initial contact with Generalexim in Hanoi bore fruit. We met Do Dinh Thi, a director of Mark's joint-venture business, whose official title is an Export Agricultural and Forest Products Processing Factory. Do Dinh Thi had a formal, governmental air that was in complete contrast to Mark's relaxed, entrepreneurial manner. Although Mark's association with Do Dinh Thi made the formation of his company possible, I detected some frustration on Mark's part when it came to government red tape. The reality here is that without the support of a state corporation and the incumbent official to rubberstamp everything, nothing would progress. Before the economic rationalists amongst us react with shock, ponder for a moment the tidal wave of regulations and paperwork that have buried small businesses in Australia in the first couple of years of the new millennium.

Travelling in Hanoi reminded us so much of travelling in India. The roads were mostly narrow, lumpy and filled with a haphazard, horn-blaring stream of push-bikes, motor scooters, trucks, pedestrians, occasional bullock carts and pony traps. Hanoi has its own distinct character too, which we realised as huge, narrow-tracked trucks with wide, curved cabins shaped like Chairman Mao's cheekbones lumbered by. Among the slow traffic, and far up into the country, a common sight was a chunky, short truck that has the appearance of having been crossed with a tractor, bearing enormous rear wheels and small, tractor-like front wheels. This utilitarian vehicle costs about A$5000 and its low-compression diesel engine chugs its way rhythmically along the dusty roads, sounding as unstoppable as a steam roller.

We were on our way to Yen Bai, about 120 kilometres north-west of Hanoi, but in this crowded traffic the drive took about five hours. To all travellers sustenance is paramount and we were delighted when we stopped to have lunch in Viet Tri City in Phu Tho province at a restaurant called Quan Ca Ben Song, which literally means 'fish restaurant by the river'. Lunch was ordered by our hosts, including bottles of beer for Liz, me and the driver (Vietnamese women do not appear to be large consumers of alcohol, however it seems the men make up for them). We thoroughly enjoyed the *ca lang* (long fish) served in three ways: roasted, fried and in soup. Our road rule of never eating uncooked greens was broken here as we tucked into a mass of greenery including coriander leaves, Vietnamese mint, dill, spiky perennial coriander leaves (*Eryngium foetidum*) and lettuce leaves. The reason behind the 'rule' (which I still consider mandatory in India) is that the water food is washed in may contain bacteria that our Western systems have little resistance to. The usual result is a dose of 'Delhi belly', the 'colly wobbles' or the 'Jimmy Brits'. Call it what you will, it is uncomfortable and downright inconvenient to have diarrhoea when travelling. We need not have worried because, as it turned out, we had not one tummy upset the whole time we were in Vietnam.

At the time of our visit to Vietnam perennial coriander was gaining popularity in Australia. Gardeners get impatient with annual coriander (*Coriandrum sativum*) because no sooner does it start growing well than it flowers, goes to seed and dies. Known in Vietnam as *ngo gai*, *mui tau* or *ngo tay*, perennial coriander is believed to be native to the Caribbean islands and is now widely cultivated in South-East Asia. We have also seen it growing at a Spices Board research station in Kerala, in the south of India. This perennial 'long coriander' has serrated leaves about 5 centimetres long, making them particularly useful here because of the Vietnamese propensity to wrap food. The aroma when crushed is similar to conventional coriander leaves, the only drawback being a slightly grassy aftertaste and sharp, spiky mouth feel. I have started using it, but tend to put the whole leaves into soups and remove them before serving. Unlike many leaves that get harder as they mature, the largest leaves of this coriander are noticeably softer than the young ones. Our meal finished with green tea and fresh mandarins. The driver showed us how rubbing one's lips with the shiny side of mandarin peel, cleans them and leaves them feeling fresh.

On the outskirts of Yen Bai the main street wound past shop-houses and villas. Rows of bang trees lined the road, their large flat leaves in browns and reds casting shade in a charming, enveloping canopy. The bang trees were very common and appeared to be no more than twenty years old, which made us wonder if they were part of a postwar replanting program. We were reluctant to ask questions like these – the old 'Don't mention the war' syndrome. When we did talk about it they always referred to it as 'the American war'. Considering we were at war until 1975, the hospitality and friendliness of the people never ceased to amaze us.

On our arrival in Yen Bai we drove down a wide main street flanked by magnificent new municipal buildings. Each one was five storeys high, painted turmeric yellow, surrounded by high wrought-iron fences and roofed in traditional French angles.

Mark had warned us that accommodation in Yen Bai might be basic. 'Although wherever you travel in Vietnam, no matter how humble the abode, there will always be a supply of disposable toothbrushes,' he had said. We were pleasantly surprised as we pulled into the carpark of a white, four-storey hotel surrounded by topiary trees in huge pots. Our room, which was really much more like a suite, must have been one of the best, for although sparse, from the hallway one went into a large living room. In the centre was a long carved table, a little higher than a coffee table, and two rows of six ornately carved chairs. In the bedroom Liz found that at each corner of the bed there were extendable rods like car radio aerials to prop up the voluminous mosquito net that was stored under the pillows.

After unpacking, our entourage sought out a little restaurant in the town that served *com pho*, which we deduced to mean 'Chinese-style rice noodle'. That is, the meal would be soup-based and accompanied by fresh greens, noodles or rice.

We were interested to find a surprising amount of dill tips among the greenery in the soup. In Australia we don't tend to think of dill (*Anethum graveolens*) as an Asian ingredient, however when one considers how well it goes with coriander leaf, pepper, cardamom, cumin and turmeric in a Kuwaiti fish stew, one need not be surprised at how good it tastes in Asian dishes. Next time you are making an Asian stir-fry or soup, try adding equal quantities of coriander leaf and dill tips. The dill gives a delightful anise-and-parsley-flavoured freshness.

By now we had spent a long day with our travelling companions and were feeling comfortable in each other's company. The young women were curious about life in Australia. We told them about our daughters, Liz producing some well-worn photos from her purse, and lamented the absence of grandchildren. We talked about our cities, the economy, our business and the hopes and aspirations of young Australians. Yen didn't speak any English (and does not need to with Mark being fluent in Vietnamese) but from her facial expressions and excited interjections in Vietnamese, we guessed she understood what we were saying. Van Anh had been working for Mark for a few years and appeared to be a very capable personal assistant. Huong was relatively new and still learning the ropes. This trip to the cassia forests was the first for both of them, and Mark felt it would be helpful in their education about the cassia trade. This pleased us, as we did feel a bit guilty about taking four of his staff away from work.

The next morning we awoke to sounds that evoked thoughts of what life must have been like during the people's revolution. Loudspeakers burst forth in the cool, pre-dawn still air. The sounds of music followed by some sort of dialogue echoed with metallic amplification at five o'clock in the morning. When it fully roused us an hour later, we thought how soothing and melodious it was and what a great way to start the next day of our adventure.

We set out early, after another *com pho* breakfast of beef soup and noodles. Today we had to get to the village of Khe Dua (pronounced 'kay zuer') further north, in the direction of the Red River that flows down from China and which we had been more or less shadowing since we came up from Hanoi. The morning's drive lasted a little over an hour and took us further away from civilisation. The villages became smaller and the building materials more basic, with walls and roofs of thatch. The expanses of paddy fields were almost overwhelming, reminding us that the country is predominantly rural.

At a little village at the end of the road we hired the trail bikes to go further up alongside the river and into the cassia forests. Knowing the track to be rough, Liz and I decided to travel pillion. Yen arranged for a few local men to drive us. We clung onto our young drivers as they took off on the sturdy 125 cc bikes made in Belarus. All of a sudden we were heading down a steep, narrow track leading to the riverbank. I hoped the soft alluvial bank would not give way and plunge us into the drink. It held and we arrived safely by the Red River where we could see a couple of flat-bottomed barges on the other side. The ferryman got out of his on-board hammock and expertly manoeuvred the steel-hulled, 6 metre long open barge over to us, judging the current to sweep it sideways just enough to moor in exactly the right spot. Our motorbikes were pushed on board over a couple of narrow, bowing planks.

We really began to realise we were on a special adventure.

Here we were on this remote stretch of the Red River, civilisation was behind us and we were surrounded by Vietnam's natural beauty. The steep, muddy climb up the other side of the riverbank was as disconcerting as the descent, only this time I was hoping my 80-plus kilos would not tip me off the back.

The next 8 kilometres were a wonderful trail bike ride along a 2 to 3 metre wide track that rose up steep embankments, passed by clear, reflective lakes and forded muddy rivulets. Occasionally we would pitch and bounce up rutted, slippery slopes and rocky, bone-jarring sections of track, our drivers never erring in their judgement. We came to a stretch of deep mud and thong-sucking ooze which required us to dismount and pick a tightrope-like track along the side, while the men slid and skidded in an exhaust-smoke haze to the other side. We teetered on our slippery side track. Losing our footing would result in stumbling into the mud or falling through a tangle of weeds into the rice paddy below.

As we rode further up the hills we passed beautiful stands of pandanus (*Pandanus amaryllifolius*), their fan-like fronds shining green and reflecting the mid-morning light in picture postcard beauty. By now we felt at home on the bikes, their hard-working two-stroke engines the only sound penetrating the stillness of the hills and the dense forest. More signs of life emerged as we came upon the small village of Khe Dua with its one main earthen track, timber houses on stilts, schoolyard and oxen pulling a cart-sized bunch of freshly cut pandanus fronds.

Khe Dua is Vietnam's largest producer of premium-grade cassia and Yen, Van Anh and Huong introduced us to the principal farmers, Dzoanh and his wife Oanh (pronounced 'Zwine' and 'Wine'). Yen visits them regularly in the harvesting season to buy cassia. As is customary in all these situations we sat down in Dzoanh and Oanh's timber house to green tea and conversation.

From the outside the house looked like a cross between a traditional, verandahless 'Queenslander' on stilts and a rural cottage. Wide timber steps where five abreast could stand to be photographed led to the front entrance 2 metres above the road. Underneath it sloped away to provide an airy 3 to 4 metre high space at the back that provided ample shelter for a ruffling of pigs and a sleepy, ruminating ox. Inside, the ceiling followed the vaulted, high pitch of the roof and generous windows let in views of the jungle, while the house was decorated with lanterns, pictures, souvenirs and ornaments.

Liz and I were captivated by Oanh, who is the daughter of the old man of the village, and her business acumen appears to have a lot to do with their success. Her charming smile and friendly eyes won us over immediately. Dzoanh was animated in his explanations about cassia and while Huong and Van Anh translated for us he would take a long, gurgling drawback on his huge bamboo pipe and expel an aromatic cloud of smoke. I never cease to be inspired by the ability we humans have to communicate with no common language but a strong commonality of interest. We discussed cassia in all its forms. Someone appeared with a leafy branch of cassia covered in cassia buds, the small, cup-shaped section that holds its fruit (a 10 millimetre, dark green, egg-shaped seed). Although not commonly eaten here, Dzoanh encouraged me to taste some. When chewed, these fresh cassia buds released a refreshing cinnamon flavour with a distinctly hot aftertaste that was lighter and sharper than the warm, comforting flavour of dried cassia bark.

I had recently heard of cassia buds being used in recipes and was anxious to find out what all the excitement was about. I must admit I am a little embarrassed by our Western over-enthusiasm for the exotic. It is not the first time I have come across some rare plant part that has become all the rage among the trendiest of chefs, only to discover the underwhelming reputation it has in its native land.

I inspected the cassia leaves closely. They appeared to be slightly darker in colour, larger and more elongated than cinnamon leaves, with two distinct ribs running lengthways either side of a straight rib from stem to tip. These leaves were also aromatic and cassia leaf oil is extracted by steam distillation and is used in products as varied as confectionery, beverages and perfumes. During our conversation in the living area of Dzoanh and Oanh's house it was pointed out to us that the 60 centimetre diameter posts, which ran from the ground to the high, vaulted ceiling, were in fact cassia logs. The bark long since stripped away, these majestic supports had acquired a deep brown patina that enhanced the welcoming atmosphere of the room. Pleasantries completed, our passports were handed to a couple of government officials who appeared stony-faced from nowhere, and are ever-present, even out here. Leaving our passports with the same trepidation one leaves a toddler at preschool for the first time, we had to get back on our bikes and ride a short distance to the cassia forest.

No more haphazard jungle but a neat, cool and shady habitat for the straight-trunked cassia trees, which ranged from four to ten years old. Cassia trees resemble the brush box trees (*Tristania conferta*) we see planted in suburban streets in Sydney. During growth the lower limbs are trimmed off to ensure smooth bark predominantly free from knot holes. A stand of cassia trees has a distinct appearance, for not only are the trunks incredibly straight, but they are blotched with pale green and almost white, evenly spaced fungal spots. The ground was lit-tered with a carpet of sienna-brown, dry leaves which are slightly aromatic and are used by the locals as odour-fighting inner soles. We selected a few size 10s to wear back to Hanoi. Several workers were raking these leaves aside and picking up small black seeds from the ground. Huong explained that these are the green fruits that we saw earlier on the branch, however they had been eaten by birds and as she said, 'When the bird shits them out they are collected to germinate.' The phenome-non of seeds germinating successfully after passing through the intestines of birds is not uncommon. The allspice trees of Jamaica are propagated this way and all over the world birds are responsible for the spread of weeds.

The bark from three cassia trees will earn enough money to build a house in Khe Dua. Cassia trees are not ready to har-vest until they are seven years old, as younger than that is not economical. Trees over eight years old attract a tax, therefore, with the exception of the occasional twenty to twenty-five-year-old tree, most are harvested at just under eight years.

Harvesting is performed in the wet seasons, March and August, when the bark is easiest to remove. Considering the value of cassia, we were privileged to be given a demonstration, because once some bark is removed the whole tree is effectively ring-barked and has to be cut down. Once felled all the remain-ing bark is stripped off.

Dzoanh picked up his knife in front of about a dozen onlookers who were more entertained by our reactions than the all too familiar bark-stripping demonstration. First he cut through the bark just above ground level. The knife blade was 25 centimetres long, with a half-arrowhead-shaped point that scored and cut the bark through to the wood as Dzoanh rotated it around the tree's circumference. This cut complete, Dzoanh measured 30 centimetres further up the trunk and repeated the process. Next he made a vertical slit joining one ring-cut to the other and using a flat, blade-like stick of bamboo, he prised the slit open and, separating bark from moist pale wood, proceeded to peel off a complete scroll of bark. The aroma released was sweet with tangy notes, like a cinnamon-spiced pie made with sharp, green apples. However like many spices the volatile oil only concentrates and becomes pungent as a result of drying, when the scroll loses half its weight and the pale inner bark turns a dark, reddish brown.

The bark-stripping process is repeated up the tree until three 30 centimetre scrolls have been removed. The naked tree is then cut down and an army of peelers will remove all the usable cassia from the upper trunk and branches. Dzoanh and Oanh made a generous gift to us of three beautiful scrolls of cassia bark tightly rolled together. Each scroll could have been wrapped around a forearm to make a play-acting plaster cast, as its proportions and weight were the same.

After the demonstration, we headed back to the house for a summing-up over more green tea. Huong had mentioned to Liz when our passports were taken that we might not be allowed to leave until late afternoon, but Yen must have done some sweet-talking about how far we had to travel home, as our passports were soon returned to us. Back at the village Yen suddenly became the most animated we had seen her. She took my hand firmly and led me along the track until we came to a magnificent twenty-five-year-old tree that had a diameter of over a metre and was at least 40 metres high. Its bark would be more than 1.5 centimetres thick and if harvested would yield in excess of a tonne of cassia.

Yen put her arms around the tree to show its size and possibly as an indication of her fondness for these trees, which are the basis of this village's livelihood. A photo session followed with us posing with different folks, all hugging the tree, each other or both. Oanh's father, the old man of the village, offered his wizened countenance to the camera, and it was a happy and joyous finale to our visit.

We re-mounted the bikes with the cassia scrolls strapped to the parcel carrier on the back of my bike. As we came around a gentle curve and headed downhill towards a quiet, glassy, noon-sunned lake, I saw a *nogood boyo* lying back in his wide, hand-made canoe and slowly rowing with his feet gripping the oars. I doubt whether I have ever seen anything so leisurely and skilled. Then the bike in front opened up its throttle, blue smoke enveloped me and we all roared up the next incline leaving *nogood boyo* back on the lagoon.

We arrived in Hanoi that evening and as Liz was pretty exhausted from the last two days she decided to have a bath, room service and an early night. I went out for dinner with Mark as it was my last chance to see him before we left Vietnam and I wanted to present him with a copy of the American edition of my book *Spice Notes* and thank him for his hospitality.

Mark was almost penniless when he came to Vietnam. Since then, he has become one of the country's major cassia exporters and a respected businessman, and has grown to really love the place. I asked him about the attitude to Americans and Australians after the war and he said, 'The great thing about the Vietnamese is that they just get on with looking to the future, all that's in the past.' He is, though, very critical of exploitative behaviour and has a highly developed sense of fairness. 'I haven't got any time for the expats who come here for a few years, booze up all the time and have a different local woman every week.' Mark is pleased that he is fluent in Vietnamese and gets his greatest pleasure when he, Yen and their little boy Haong are together as a family.

Only a few weeks before we left Australia for Vietnam there was an article in the travel section of the *Sun-Herald* about the old town of Hoi An, east of Danang in between Ho Chi Minh City and Hanoi. The attraction of Hoi An is that it was untouched by the bombing during the war and many old buildings are still standing. So we decided to go there and have a couple of days rest and recreation on the way back to Sydney. We booked into the Victoria Hoi An Resort with some trepidation, as the last resort we had stayed in was the one in Dar es Salaam on our way to Zanzibar.

To our great relief we arrived at a dream come true. There was clear, blue ocean on one side and lake and rice paddies on the other. The grounds of the resort were beautifully laid out and we were sorely tempted to veg out there and not bother exploring the town. While checking in, we noticed an elephant waving its trunk up towards the reception balcony. Darling, a tame female elephant, would wander around the tables in the courtyard at breakfast time and occasionally go and scratch her tummy on one of the balustrades. We hoped they were solid.

Of course, we did explore the town, looking up the sights described in the newspaper article such as the sixteenth-century covered Japanese bridge and the colonnaded, French-looking streetscape in Phan Boi Chau Street. We had iced coffee by the Thu Bon River, which had been a major trading port until it silted up and large ships had to sail to Danang. As we sat by the clear water, we tried to imagine what it must have been like here in the tenth century when it was a bustling seaport just 5 kilometres from the South China Sea. Persian and Arab documents from that era mention Hoi An as a provisioning stop for sailing ships, and no doubt many spice traders had ventured through here over the centuries.

Arriving back in Sydney I was very polite to the quarantine man who thought I must have been some kind of idiot wanting to bring three scrolls of cassia bark into the country. But one smell of the cassia convinced him that I was onto a good thing. However it had to be heat-treated to kill any insects, larvae or eggs that might be in the bark. With all the appropriate forms filled in, fees paid and delivery instructions given, we were told to expect our treated goods back in about three weeks.

On my desk sits a 45 centimetre long, 5 centimetre diameter scroll of cassia bark from Khe Dua. I feel its rough outer texture, look at its smooth, rich brown core that was white when freshly peeled from the tree, and smell its heady fragrance. I am transported to the cassia forests, the Red River, Oanh's sparkling smile and I thank another spice brother, Mark, for making the whole experience possible.

JOURNEY to the
CENTRE of AUSTRALIA

In the last decade or so there has been a lot of interest in the commercial opportunities provided by our own edible Australian native plants (often referred to as 'bush tucker'), including those used as spices. Most non-indigenous people would perish quickly in the outback without adequate supplies of familiar, life-sustaining produce. The Aboriginal people, however, have lived for countless generations in apparently barren areas because they know where to find the varied and abundant foods, and how to prepare them. The Australian government, through the Rural Industries Research and Development Corporation (RIRDC), is supporting the bush food industry by encouraging the development of markets for these native foods both here and abroad. For years now, many restaurateurs around Australia have been experimenting and bringing the wonders of native flavours to Australians and tourists alike. Yet with all this interest and support, households and restaurants are still reluctant to make regular use of the so-called 'bush foods'.

There are a few possible reasons for this. First, unlike conventional herbs and spices, Australia's native spices have a sketchy history of being used as seasonings. Indigenous people use them for sustenance and for their medicinal and spiritual properties, but I was only aware of a few examples of Australian native spices being traditionally used to flavour food.

Another reason is that Australian native spices bear the burden of gimmick appeal. Gimmick value has helped to generate awareness here and overseas, but the whole idea of 'bush foods' is at odds with the way consumers see themselves preparing everyday meals. Although Australians might watch the Bush Tucker Man eating witchetty grubs, strange leaves and pods on their television screens, they are unlikely to relate his experiences to their own diets. A third barrier to the success of these indigenous flavours relates to the cooking methods required for a lot of our Australian spices. Many have delicate, fresh top notes that cannot sustain long cooking, or when used in too large a quantity leave an unpleasant camphor taste in the food. A basic understanding of how to use these spices will overcome this problem. After all, you can imagine the result of using too much pepper, chilli, cardamom or cloves in a meal. The skills that we have acquired through generations of traditional spice use can be applied equally to these native flavours so that eventually using akudjura (*Solanum centrale*) or lemon myrtle (*Backhousia citriodora*) becomes no more mysterious than adding chilli or lemongrass.

While there are hundreds of bush foods that can sustain

life, my interest focused on the varieties that can be used to flavour food. Of particular interest to me has been a variety of bush tomato we call akudjura, which grows in the spinifex sandplains, sandhills and mulga country of Central Australia. I use akudjura quite a lot, have researched and written about it, but had never seen it growing or being harvested. My mission, therefore, was to travel to Central Australia and see it for myself. In the same manner as many culinary herbs and spices are gathered around the world, the bulk of akudjura is gathered from the wild, a process often referred to as wildcrafting. I was fortunate enough to be seated next to Andrew Fielke at the Tasting Australia awards dinner in 2001. Andrew started a restaurant in Adelaide called Red Ochre, where he worked his own special alchemy with Australian native foods. When I mentioned my desire to track down akudjura and see it growing, he said, 'You need to go to the Centre and see the bush tomato queen. Her name is Janet Chisholm and she and her husband Roy own Napperby Station, about 200 kilometres north-west of Alice Springs.' Andrew emailed Janet's contact details to me and my hunt for akudjura began.

When I contacted Janet she said it would be best to visit in early April the following year, after the wet season and when we would still be able to find some akudjura on the plants. So on 2 April 2002 I flew from Sydney to Alice Springs, having made arrangements to hire a four-wheel drive. I was returning in just two days, and knowing I had some hundreds of kilometres to travel, prayed that this shortest of excursions would be successful.

As the plane was landing at Alice Springs, I was surprised at how green the countryside looked. After two good wet seasons the red desert had been transformed. I collected the four-wheel drive and set off. Before leaving Sydney Janet had given me directions: 'Drive north from Alice for 120 kilometres and then turn west and drive for 80 kilometres. See you on Tuesday afternoon.' In the blink of an eye I had driven into Alice Springs, bought a couple of bottles of water and was out of town and on the Stuart Highway to Darwin. The sense of exhilaration at driving into the most enormous blue sky on Earth, reminded me of when we arrived back in Australia after spending nearly a year in Singapore. We'd gone to stay with friends near Cowra, and after the hemmed-in hustle and bustle and high-rises of Asia's most progressive city, we felt as if a huge burden had been peeled away from our souls leaving us refreshed, renewed and cleansed.

The first 120 kilometres of road was excellent and it was no effort to cruise at 110 km/h through the wide, flat landscape. Just before turning west I passed an impressive rocky outcrop at Nature Gap that rose majestically from the surrounding plains. The next 80 kilometres were all red dust and corrugations, termite nests standing like sentinels among the sparse, grey-green vegetation. The road narrowed as the odometer indicated I was nearly 200 kilometres from Alice Springs. I'd made good time and after landing at Alice just over two hours before, I was approaching the homestead on Napperby Station.

Janet was as I had imagined her to be from the brief telephone conversations and emails we had exchanged – no-nonsense and hyperactive. She and her husband Roy run one of the largest privately owned cattle stations in the Northern Territory. Over a million acres, with an Aboriginal community of over 300, a general store adjoining the homestead and a road-house at Tillmouth Well some 40 kilometres away, no wonder she has to be able to do at least three things at once. An enormous kettle was put on the Aga fuel stove and over a cup of tea Janet outlined what we would be doing that afternoon.

An old lady had recently died in the community, so the women who would be showing us the *kudjura*, as it's called, would be camping on the creekbed having 'sorry' in respect for their departed friend. Aboriginal mourning is referred to as 'sorry business', and about a week before relatives of the deceased had set up camp in the dry creekbed near their homes. We drove down to collect them from a spot where a stand of cut gum tree branches was pushed into the sand for shade. They were surrounded by all manner of possessions – mattresses, clothes, blankets and a motley collection of dogs. Dogs are invaluable to keep one cosy if you're camping out on the cold nights where the temperature can drop to about 12 degrees centigrade at this time of year. Hence the terms 'three-dog night' and 'two-dog night' are used in reference to the number of dogs required to keep warm.

Janet explained how when someone dies there is a traditional send-off. The community paints up and performs dances and returns the spirit of the deceased to the earth, where they believe it will rejuvenate the land. The next stage is the 'sorry business' when everyone who knew the person comes to sit with the relatives. I got the impression they don't say much, perhaps they don't need to. Janet took the hand of the husband of the dead lady, a white-haired old man of about seventy. Partially blind and too emotional to speak, he held her hand for some time as she comforted him in respectful silence. When the sorry business is complete a conventional funeral and burial are performed.

Janet had a chat with the four middle-aged women who were going to show me where they gather the akudjura. I was introduced to the two Kittys (Kitty Cockatoo and Kitty Paltoru), Jessie Forester and Nancy Naraboola, women with gentle handshakes and kind eyes, their dark, furrowed brows and skin weathered from years in the harshest of environments.

We came to a claypan, which was about a kilometre in diameter. Driving across its pale, smooth, salt-impregnated surface was suddenly quiet, like the best stretch of road you have ever travelled on, then just as quickly we were back in the scrub. A few kilometres further on we approached an area that had been ravaged by fire the season before, creating ideal conditions for a crop of *kudjura*. I was amazed to see the number of raisin-sized fruits on each small bush sprouting defiantly out of hard red soil in an incredibly prickly landscape. Everything seemed prickly; grass seeds stitched themselves into my trousers and socks like needles. The women walked off in different directions, barefoot and totally immersed in the task of *kudjura* collecting.

It was a thrill to be out in the centre of Australia on this hot afternoon, the air so dry that everything was crisp to the touch, and the sky so big and blue it was almost too intense to look at. All around me were bush tomato shrubs. Some were poisonous but there was also the edible akudjura, which is sometimes called bush tomato or desert raisin. A relative to the potato and tomato, it is a hardy perennial with woody stems that have long, sharp spikes at 5 to 8 centimetre intervals. Soft, down-covered, grayish-green leaves and young, rust-coloured leaves set off attractive violet flowers with yellow stamens, each in the shape of a five-pointed star. The elder Kitty showed me some unripe fruits that were around 2 centimetres in diameter and pale green. These ripen to pale yellow and as the sticky fruits dry on the bush, they shrink to 1.5 or 1 centimetre, the colour darkens to chocolate brown and a chewy, raisin-like consistency develops. Kitty pointed to the unripe ones and said, 'Cheeky!' and shook her finger. Janet explained that anything that is 'cheeky' is inedible and might make you sick. I nibbled on some dry ones that Kitty assured me were okay. The fruits are allowed to dry naturally on the plant before gathering, a process that is essential if they are to be safely eaten with no harmful side-effects – this is because during the drying process, the level of alkaloids is reduced. Dehydration also concentrates the flavours in akudjura and creates more full-bodied and com-plex flavour notes, in the same way as many familiar spices (cloves, pepper, allspice) develop their flavour only after being dried in the sun. Akudjura has a distinct, pleasant, 'caramel mingled with sun-dried tomato' aroma with comforting 'baked' background notes reminiscent of an Anzac biscuit. About 30 seconds after biting into one the flavour becomes somewhat bitter, and there is a lingering aftertaste which leaves the palate unexpectedly refreshed.

I stood there in a part of the world that probably looked no different thousands of years ago, nibbled on akudjura and thought that this may be among the oldest of spices known to the human race. Native to Central and Western Australia, akudjura has a strong connection with the beliefs of the Warlpiri and Anmatyerr peoples of Central Australia. Like many Australian native plants, members of the *solanum* family thrive after bushfires, then the initial prolific fruiting steadily declines over a few years until rejuvenated by the next bushfire.

The Aboriginal people have used fire judiciously to manage the productivity of food-producing plants for generations. Many Australian trees regenerate after fire and the seeds of countless grasses and native food plants will only germinate after being subjected to fire, so much so that areas which have not been systematically subjected to fire become devoid of food-bearing vegetation.

The Aborigines once regarded akudjura as a staple. It was gathered and ground with water to produce a thick paste, which was formed into large balls and left to dry in the blazing sun. The high acidity, characterised by the tangy flavour and rich vitamin C content, acted as a preservative, making storage over long periods possible. These balls of akudjura were often wedged into the forks of trees, making them readily available to eat later. The unique flavour of akudjura is best appreciated when used in small quantities, as using too much will cause the bitter sharp notes to dominate and leave the fruity, sweet, caramel flavours masked to the palate. Whole akudjura can be added to long, slow-cooked dishes such as soups and casseroles. Powdered akudjura gives a baked taste to sweet biscuits and apple crumble. I have found it combines particularly well with ground coriander seed, wattleseed (*Acacia aneura*), lemon myrtle and a little salt for rubbing onto white and red meats before grilling, barbecuing or stir-frying. A tangy pepper steak spice can be made by pounding black and white peppercorns, mustard seeds, salt and akudjura in a pestle and mortar, then sprinkled over the steak and barbecued. I also like to put this mix on tomato sandwiches instead of pepper and salt.

Kitty the elder, the most knowledgeable and talkative of the four women, drew my attention to another variety of bush tomato (*Solanum chippendalei*). The bush was almost identical to akudjura, however it bore shiny, round, green fruits 3 centimetres in diameter suspended from a large, spiky, elf-cap-shaped calyx. Kitty cut one in half and scraped out the mass of shiny black seeds and inner skin, then invited me to taste the honeydew melon-like flesh. The taste was bland, vaguely reminiscent of rockmelon and quite underwhelming. She explained how they threaded halves of this bush tomato onto skewers of desert rose sticks to dry them.

The danger of gathering native foods without expert advice was made abundantly apparent to me when Kitty pointed to another bush tomato plant (*Solanum quadriloculatum*) with seemingly identical flowers and green fruits with a spongy texture. 'Cheeky, emu and kangaroo eat,' she said. This plant, so similar in appearance to akudjura except for its larger, sage-like leaves and green fruit, is extremely poisonous and should definitely be avoided.

The women were particularly excited to find some *kirliyi*, the native tobacco bush (*Duboisia hopwoodii*), which is also called the pituri bush or 'emu poison'. The emu poison name derives from its use as poison in waterholes where emus were known to drink. The poisoned, comatose emu would then be an easy kill. It is believed that although poisonous to birds and stock, the water can be drunk by humans after a few days with no reported ill effects. The narcotic content of nicotine in this plant makes it popular as chewing tobacco.

A couple of hours passed quickly with the women each gathering a small tin filled with *kudjura* and armfuls of *kirliyi*. I shot off two rolls of film, taking close-ups and different angles of every fruit-bearing shrub, much to the amusement of the others. We piled back into the vehicle and headed to the creekbed. On the way the women wanted to show me the witchetty bushes (*Acacia kempeana*) where they get witchetty grubs. The only problem was they needed a 'crowb' (crowbar) to dig them up. Janet suggested getting a crowb and returning, however they were now more interested in going back to the creekbed for 'sorry'. So we called it a day and agreed to collect them in the morning to look for witchetty grubs.

Dinner that evening was roast beef off the property which was dry marinated earlier with a rub of ground coriander seeds, wattleseed, akudjura, lemon myrtle, mountain pepperleaf (*Tasmannia lanceolata*) and salt.

The Napperby beast provided a delicious dinner and, over animated conversation, it turned out that the Chisholms and I had a number of mutual acquaintances, reconfirming what a small world it really is. It seemed hard to believe that just that morning I was getting on a plane in Sydney and in the following twelve hours had travelled to the centre of the continent and seen and learnt so much. The evening air was cool, the sky brilliant with stars and the night clear and quiet. I wrote up as much as I could remember in my notebook and then slept like a log.

The morning was quiet, still and cool. The spinifex was as dry as parchment and cast long, spindly shadows in the slanting, early light. Birds called in intermittent tweets, in the distance a larger bird honked and the only sound of a human presence was the distant humming of a generator. Breakfast was quick. Roy had a crane loaded aboard a semitrailer low loader, as he was off to repair one of the thirty windmills on the property. He was taking Lucy, Janet's stocky little black dog, for company. A truckload of supplies was arriving soon from Alice and would have to be unloaded, and about a tonne of akudjura would have to be put on pallets to be taken back to a transport company in Alice Springs.

I made myself useful by stacking the 50 kilo boxes of akudjura and addressing them to a customer in Melbourne who makes a range of sauces and condiments with native flavours. Janet unloaded the supply truck, assisted by Karen, who looks after the station's general store and two young women on a working holiday from England. The station homestead and its outbuildings resemble a tiny town. North of the homestead, across a wide, dirt track that could be the main street from a *High Noon* western, are the guests' quarters, the butchery, jackeroos' accommodation and Roy's office. Less than 100 metres from the homestead, on the other side of the thirty-tree citrus orchard and Janet's vegetable garden is the general store that is used by the Napperby Aboriginal community and stockmen who work on the station. It is a brown, corrugated-iron shed, divided into four sections. The main store part is a little bigger than a double garage, its shelves crammed with every conceivable need: clothes, food, car batteries, tyres, toys, ghetto blasters, soft drinks, chips, long-life milk and custard. A bathroom-sized freezer room is filled with ice-cream, frozen goods and crushed ice. Two storerooms are filled with soft drinks, biscuits and snackfoods. Off to one side is the takeaway food area.

As the day warmed the wakening activity intensified. Jackeroos came and went. The morning's chores completed and the tabletop truck loaded, we collected Kitty Cockatoo, Jessie and Nancy from their sorry vigil at the creekbed and drove a short distance south-west to find some witchetty bushes. This time each of them had a crowb, an easily handled steel bar about a metre and a half long. One end has a pointed tip and the other is flattened, like the tip of a conventional crowbar. We soon reached a good scattering of witchetty bushes, not too difficult as they are widespread throughout this region. These bushes were about 2 metres high, although they can grow to 4 metres, and had a dense crown of foliage on ten or more stems that rose from the ground. What makes the witchetty bush so important to the Aboriginal people is the protein in the fat grubs that can be found in their roots. The grubs are the larvae of a large grey moth (*Xyleutes biarpiti*) that emerges from the roots in the warmer months after heavy rain.

Finding the witchetty grubs was an art in itself. The women prodded their crowbars into the soil around the base of the scrubby bushes until they heard the metal hit a root. Not just any root, but one that gave a certain hollow sound when struck, indicating that a grub was inside. Kitty then dug, poked and prised at the ground until a distended root about 20 centimetres long and 2 centimetres in diameter was pulled up. The swollen appearance of the root, and the plug of frass that could be seen, bode well for a successful harvest. Sitting on the ground, Kitty proceeded to chip at the root with the flat end of her crowb until a pale, soft grub appeared. She delicately grabbed it between thumb and forefinger and extracted 5 centimetres of almost white grub. As thick as a forefinger, these nutritious morsels are lightly roasted on hot coals and taste distinctly nutty with egg yolk overtones. Kitty had found a particularly prolific bush and she went on to dig up another ten grubs, depositing them in her tin.

Nancy pointed to a tangled, spiny shrub nearby that was

covered in small, shiny green and black berries less than 5 millimetres in diameter. I made sure that they weren't cheeky before
tasting the pleasantly sweet flesh. Called conkerberry (*Carissa
brownii*), this plant is most commonly found in these woodland
areas north of Alice Springs. As I tucked into them with a gusto
that reminded me of collecting blackberries as a kid, Janet
warned me that eating too many can make you very thirsty. I
wondered why I had not seen them among other bush foods
that have made their way to the cities, and discovered that as
well as growing in a limited area, the plant only fruits for about
three weeks of the year. Apparently the dried berries may be
gathered from the ground around the shrub and then soaked in
water before being eaten.

When we dropped Kitty, Jessie and Nancy back at the
dry creekbed, I thanked them for their kindness in sharing their
knowledge with me. We got their crowbs out of the back of the
vehicle, shook hands and parted at a pace that was seemingly
more respectful than the speedy dismissals we give to people in
the city.

My next destination was the Yuendumu community in
the north-west, to visit Frank Baarda, whom Janet had kindly
arranged for me to meet. Janet farewelled me, giving directions
to Tillmouth Well, which I'd stop at on the way. 'Just follow
the creek, keeping it on your left and when you get to Tanami
Road, you'll see the roadhouse on your left. Don't forget to
refuel before heading off to Yuendumu and give Frank my
regards.' Tillmouth Well Roadhouse is aptly named as an oasis
on the Tanami. The adjacent creekbed is surrounded by magnificent, white-trunked river gums. Its utilitarian cabins are
fringed by what must be the largest expanse of green lawn for

hundreds of square miles and it even boasts a swimming pool. Reg and Rae Paterson manage the roadhouse. A couple of years ago they decided to travel around Australia and not spend more than six months in any one place. Sixteen months later they are still here. Rae phoned Frank and told him I was on my way and to expect me in around two hours, the time it would take to drive the 100 kilometres to Yuendumu. Rae told me to phone on my way back and to try to return before nightfall as night driving increases the danger of hitting kangaroos, stock or even camels in the dark.

The Tanami Track is the quickest way to get from south-eastern Australia to the Kimberley in the north-west. It passes through some of the most sparsely populated areas of the continent, and even though the road is being improved, the area is remote and dangerous. When travelling alone you are obliged to report your position and let people know when you expect to arrive at your destination.

So, with filled waterbottles, some trepidation and a welling sense of excitement I drove onto the 1 kilometre strip of sealed road, bounced off it onto the dirt, pushed the Landcruiser up to 100 km/h and headed north-west in a cloud of red dust. The first stop I made was to take a photo of the Stuart Bluff Range, a jumbled pile of red-oxide and natural, ochre-coloured rock debris that looked as though it had been constructed by ancient artisans. Every now and then I passed a car wreck, the cost of retrieving it, no doubt, far in excess of its value. In the hot, clear, early afternoon the sky was still unbelievably enormous. A faint spiral of smoke wound skyward as I drove through the area known as the Yalpirakinu. Heat haze flooded the road, as if I could plunge into cool shimmering water a few kilometres ahead. To my right the Ngalurbindi Hills south of Mount Allan could be seen in the distance. I came across three other vehicles travelling in the opposite direction and we each lifted a finger from the steering wheel in a subdued wave. Funny how in isolation we greet another motorist, but try to merge into a lane approaching the Sydney Harbour Bridge and you're more likely to see a different finger lifted at you!

I arrived at Yuendumu by two in the afternoon and proceeded to look for Frank. Hot, sparse piles of rubbish, car wrecks, dust, graffiti, rusty corrugated iron, and dogs were my first impressions of the community. I drove around asking for Frank, pulled up at a general store and fuel station and wound down the window. A tall, scruffy white man with a few days' stubble on his face, bare feet and crystal-clear blue eyes said, 'You must be looking for Frank?' to which I replied, 'That's right.' 'Well you've just found him then, park over there and I'll be with you in a minute.' I parked and bought a soft drink from the store and waited while Frank finished the conversation he was having with a chap who I think was a mining engineer. The hot sun burned through the corrugated-iron awning of the store verandah and just as Frank's conversation was winding up, a spiralling, eye-stinging dust-devil swept past us, enveloped us in a dusty shroud and was gone just as quickly as it came.

Frank cut straight to the chase. Having been briefed by Janet, he knew I was after information about the bush foods he is involved in. However I soon found out that this fascinating geologist was a wealth of information on many subjects, and I was only sorry that I could not have spent longer with him. Frank had come to this area as an exploration geologist, and in one of those life-changing moments made his home here. We went into one of his offices behind the shop, where piles of paper, bits of machinery, and goodness knows what littered the room, as if a dozen dust-devils had just cycloned through it. The first thing he did was plonk a book down in front of me called *Bushfires and Bushtucker: Aboriginal plant use in Central Australia* by Peter Latz and say, 'It's printed by the Institute of Aboriginal Affairs in Alice Springs, you'll have to get a copy from their bookshop in Alice.' I did, and I would highly recommend it to anyone who wants to know more about this subject.

Frank is the manager of the Yuendumu mining company (YMC). It is an Aboriginal owned and directed company that was incorporated in 1969 to explore and mine in the Tanami region. The YMC believes the Aboriginal people have a lot to offer the mining industry by actually participating in it on their traditional lands. To their credit, YMC has a sympathetic environmental policy and acknowledges the aspirations and opinions of Aboriginal people. So I asked Frank, 'How did a mining company become involved with native foods?'

The story starts with wattleseed (*Acacia aneura*), the variety most often used for culinary purposes. Frank began by telling me how the root system of acacia trees can go down to 30 metres. He said, 'People plant acacia trees, water them and look after them and wonder why they grow so slowly at the beginning. Above the ground they may appear slow to start, but as desert plants, they are actually sending down roots as an insurance policy for the future.' The geologist in him could not resist telling me how he found this out and he launched into a fascinating story about gold prospecting and acacia trees.

Apparently gold prospectors now have equipment that

is so sensitive it can measure what is called a 'gold value' in minute proportions, as low as some parts per billion. They discovered gold values at the surface that indicated there might be gold deposits, however 10 metres below the surface there was none. When an exploratory bore was put down, gold was discovered at 30 metres below the ground, and interestingly so were fossilised roots of acacia trees. The puzzle was then solved. The roots of the acacia trees had transported minute amounts of gold to their leaves. This had accumulated over centuries and had left this small, discernible gold value on the surface of the ground. And who says money doesn't grow on trees? The other snippet of information that I found equally fascinating was that arsenic is present in high concentrations with gold, and is one of the key indicators of the presence of gold. But there was no arsenic with the surface gold value. The acacia tree has the ability not to take up the arsenic present in the deposit because it is poisonous.

Thus, what got Frank and the community into the production of acacia seeds (wattleseed) was an enquiry from Iran requesting 1 tonne of viable acacia seeds, at a value of around A$30,000, for planting in the desert. Iran was experiencing serious problems with shifting sand dunes that were constantly on the move and engulfing villages in the process. They had begun to dig great swathes with D9 bulldozers, spray them with bitumen to retain moisture and plant acacia seeds. The magnificent root systems of these plants would then hold the dunes. The only problem was that the Iran–Iraq war broke out and by the time the seed source had been identified and sufficient quantities amassed to export, there was no market for the seeds in Iran.

With a tonne of wattleseed on their hands, Frank and other members of the community investigated alternative uses for seeds from a number of acacias. The type of wattleseed that can be eaten comes from a relatively small number of varieties of acacia trees that bear edible seed pods. There are over 700 species of acacia, and the majority have poisonous seeds, so one must be absolutely sure the variety being eaten is not cheeky. One kind that is considered as a 'food wattle' is mulga (*Acacia aneura*), whose seeds are nutritious. Frank showed me a stack of drums that were full of the shiny, dark brown seeds that look a bit like linseeds. They have little flavour in this form, but when they are roasted and ground to a grainy powder they resemble ground coffee and have a distinct, light, coffee-like aroma and pleasing, slightly bitter, nutty taste.

Mulga trees are thoroughly unlikely looking members of the pea family (*Leguminosae*) until one sees their pea-like pods, which contain seeds typical of legumes. Many acacias do not have leaves at all, but stalks that are flattened to a leaf-like shape and act as leaves, their structure making them resistant to prolonged drought. Although I didn't see any, Janet had told me about a parasitic insect that attacks mulga, causing swollen lumps to appear on its branches. These are sweet and juicy inside and are referred to as mulga apples.

Acacias have a special significance for Australians as it is the blossom of the golden wattle (*Acacia pycnantha*) that has been adopted as the nation's floral emblem. I was interested to learn that acacias are indigenous to Africa, Asia and America as well, but it is Australia's acacias that are the most decorative, bursting into fluffy, glowing masses of blossoms ranging from creamy-white to the most vibrant of yellows. Acacias were called wattle in eighteenth-century Australia because the early colonists built houses using the thin branches and trunks as framework covered by mud and clay, a method of construction known in Europe as 'wattle and daub'.

The Aboriginal people have understood the nutritional benefits of wattleseed for thousands of years and have used the seeds, roots and bark of various types of acacia for medicinal purposes. Acacia gum, which oozes from cracks in the bark, can be sucked like a lolly or soaked in water to make a kind of jelly. Dark gums are mostly astringent and unpalatable while the paler, golden-hued resins have quite an agreeable taste. Wattle bark was recognised as an important source of tannin and by the end of the nineteenth century up to 20,000 tonnes of bark were being exported to Europe and the United States for use in the leather-tanning industry. It is in cooking that wattleseed comes into its own, though, and that is what got Frank and the Yuendumu Mining Company into the food business. Wattleseed flavours sweet dishes such as ice-creams, sorbets and chocolate mousse. It can also be added to yoghurt, cheesecakes and whipped cream in much the same way as we add the tiny, sticky seeds scraped from a vanilla bean. It is delicious when mixed into pancake batter and goes well in dough for making breads.

Wattleseed complements chicken, lamb and fish, especially when a small amount is blended with ground coriander seed, a pinch of lemon myrtle leaf and salt to taste. Sprinkle this over the food before cooking – it is particularly delicious with tuna or salmon steaks and red meat – and then pan-fry, grill or barbecue the food. The wattleseed adds a subtle barbecued note that is far more appealing to the Australian palate than the popular American hickory-smoke flavour, which always seems artificial-tasting by comparison. It surprises me that no enterprising flavour company has made a wattleseed extract for the food industry to use in sauces or snackfoods.

Frank sent me an email a couple of weeks after I returned to Sydney answering my questions about the Aborigines using native spices to flavour food. Frank's wife Wendy is Warlpiri and she had pointed out that Warlpiri people are very fussy about the type of wood used for cooking. Mulga (*Acacia aneura*) is the absolute favourite and apparently specific wood types are preferred for cooking certain foods. Frank said he had noticed this when he attended a barbecue in Melbourne where odourless coals were used. In his words: 'The Melbourne barbecue seemed a bit pointless to me after having got used to eating terrific tasting meat, cooked on mulga wood coals.' Although I have not been able to glean much detail about native flavours used to spice foods, Frank told me that Wendy also mentioned a small 'vapourub-like' plant called *munyu partni-partni* (*Centipeda minima*). The strongly flavoured, small red seeds used to be collected and added to other, easier-to-collect seeds to enhance the taste of the resulting *ngurlu* (stone ground flour). Perhaps its slight narcotic properties – it had been used when native tobacco was not available – may have been another incentive for adding it to food.

Before I left for Tillmouth Well we discussed how the Aboriginal sense of time was so different from that of Europeans. Time, it seems to me, rules our lives and I cannot help but envy those who hold it in an entirely different perspective. If only I could spend a week here and not think about the plane I had to catch back to Sydney the next day.

The drive back to Tillmouth Well was incident free, the

sun was behind me now, changing the tonality of the landscape. Before dinner I browsed through the roadhouse art gallery for about an hour and bought a painting called *Women Business Dancing* by one of the Napperby artists, Beatrice. It seemed appropriate for me, as with a wife and three daughters, 'Women Business' has occupied more than half of my life! It is a delightful and masterfully executed dot painting. Serpent-like swirls dance across its metre-and-a-half length, geometric groups of dot-lines run off at angles and half-moon shapes complete the borders. It is a combination of browns, ochres, yellows, Namatjira blues, purples, rust reds and desert-flower pinks. Witchetty grub-dotted white lines appear across the picture. It is in our living room, serving as a constant reminder of the intrinsic individuality and artistic talent residing within the heart of the outback.

Rae's interest in food and spices gave me a delightful surprise at dinner. Can you imagine how thrilled the weary and dusty traveller must be when confronted by a menu that boasts: barramundi in parchment, local yabbies, outback crusted beef fillet, tanami beef, a delicately spiced satay chicken followed by home-made desserts? Although I didn't have the capacity to sample everything, the food was delicious. Walking to my cabin I took in the night sky, crystal clear, the stars burning more brightly than you ever see when diluted by pollution, lights and the loom of the city.

The next morning I watched the new day dawning. It is fascinating how the dawn in each part of the world has its own character. In the north of India, the sun climbs out of a thick haze of pollution, cooking smells fill the air and traffic sounds build to a crescendo. At the beach, a clean, bright orb rises from the teal sea through a morning salt mist. In Sydney one hears the first curfew-ending planes and eventually the sun appears above roof lines, sirens howl and birds twitter in dense suburban gardens. The morning clouds out here were thin, grey wisps with bright, burnished copper undersides. They turned to reflected gold before burning off in the intensity of the rising sun to reveal an enormous sky. Birds swooped and called frantically as if they had to get in as many last minute screeches as possible before the heat of the day silenced them. A group of thirty or more pink and grey galahs strutted noisily around the lawn, raised comb-feathers at each other and practised circus tricks on swaying power lines. Four peahens joined the fray and rushed a group of galahs, scattering them in a noisy cloud that descended to walk again, clown-like, on another patch of lawn a few metres away. I thought what a pity it is for those of us who sleep in and miss this.

I had a quick, light breakfast and hit the road. I had to travel 200 kilometres back to Alice Springs, find the Institute of Aboriginal Affairs (IAD) bookshop, buy a copy of *Bushfires and Bushtucker* and be on the midday flight back to Sydney. A southerly wind had come up and there was a light, cool breeze. I saw something up ahead that looked like animals by the roadside and as I got closer I thought they were vultures, broad, bony-shouldered and hunched over a kangaroo carcass. When I was just 50 metres from them, they lazily flew off, and then I saw that they were seven magnificent eagles.

Shortly after that I noticed a billowing cloud way up ahead and guessed that it must be a road train. The approaching vehicle, with its own gigantic dust storm swirling around it, was eerie. I decided to slow right down, having no idea whether there would be any visibility once I reached it. As soon as the bullbar of the prime mover passed me I was plunged into nil visibility and prayed that the road under me was not going to do anything unpredictable. I counted four trailers hitched together as it roared past. Then the dust began to clear, I could see ahead again and in five minutes there was no trace of the road train in the rearview mirror, nor any puffs of dust left suspended in the air.

It was difficult to imagine that I had seen so much in a little more than two days. I will always remember the feeling of peace in the wide open desert and my delight at seeing the akudjura bushes and witchetty grubs. Again the generosity and goodwill from people who are willing to share is encouraging. I can see myself approaching the use of our own native flavours with renewed enthusiasm. When I arrived back at the shop Liz told me how she had just completed an order for our Native Barbecue Spice Blend to be sent to Italy, with the labels printed in Italian. Pasta and akudjura, anyone?

EPILOGUE
TILTING at WINDMILLS

In October 1995, after visiting the Papantla vanilla farm, we stopped over in Spain on our way to a conference in London. We had heard about the annual saffron festival that is held in a little town called Consuegra, on the plains of La Mancha, and we wanted to see it. I was working for a multinational food company in Australia at that time, and as we had recently launched the first major distribution of saffron into supermarkets, I thought I should learn as much as I could about it. We only had just enough time to fly into Madrid, catch the train to Toledo, hire a car to drive to Consuegra, go back to Toledo for another night and depart for London the next day.

Liz and I had exchanged faxes with a saffron merchant in Madrid and we were under the impression that the plans for us to visit what is possibly one of the most fascinating food festivals on the planet, were well under way. When we phoned his office in Madrid when we arrived at the airport, however, we were told that he had left for the weekend and would not be back until Monday. As we were flying to London on Sunday night, and my voice was probably sounding slightly hysterical, his secretary reluctantly gave me his home number. By the time we worked out how to buy our ticket to Toledo, we ran down the steps to the platform only to get an excellent view of the back of the train as it pulled out of the station.

The next three hours were spent on the platform, desolate but resolute. 'Why even bother going to Consuegra?' Liz said pragmatically. We had booked into a hotel in Toledo and even if we didn't get to Consuegra we would find Toledo worth the visit.

The hotel was medieval and beautiful. It smelt of old stone. When I looked out over the ancient buildings, I thought that it must have been just the same in Don Quixote's time. The colours of the surrounding roofs were of every earthy hue imaginable.

We strolled around the town and soaked up the atmosphere, but it was difficult to fully enjoy what was on offer with one's mind preoccupied with finding saffron. We saw some for sale for tourists that had a very high proportion of style attached and wondered why, with all the hoo-ha about Spanish saffron, such a low grade was on display.

Finally we raised the Madrid trader at his home, and he was most apologetic about not being at his office. He said he would try to get hold of someone whom we could meet in Consuegra. That was the last we heard from him and so after a fruitless Saturday we hired a car and driver on Sunday morning, went to the plains of La Mancha and kept tilting at windmills.

Every Spaniard we met was interrogated about the whereabouts of saffron. 'Azafran?' we would ask, only to be told that the season had been so poor that there was a very small harvest this year and the festival had been cancelled. Late on Sunday morning we were still asking whomever we could try to communicate with until an English couple approached us and said, 'We hope you don't think we are rude, but we couldn't help overhearing the conversation you were having about saffron.' They went on to explain how they spend nearly half the year in Spain and understand the language pretty well. 'From what we could gather, especially from their tone of voice, we reckon they are trying to hide something from you and don't want you to see how good the harvest is. Are you in the trade?' they asked. 'Because if you are, our guess is they want you to think the supply is scarce so you'll pay more from your supplier.'

It was one of the first times I had experienced such a dead-end on my spice travels; perhaps we had been unusually lucky in the past. We resolved to put saffron out of our minds for the rest of the day and just enjoy the experience of being at La Mancha.

As fate would have it, a year after opening Herbie's Spices we began importing a beautiful, sweet, smoked Spanish paprika from a company in Murcia, a hot, dry area in south-eastern Spain that is ideally suited to citrus, grape and paprika production. The city of Murcia was formerly a Muslim kingdom in the eleventh and twelfth centuries, its inhabitants coming from north Africa. They must have felt quite at home in the heat. The owner of the company, Pepe Sanchez, has visited Australia a number of times and we love his warmth, energy and bombastic personality. On his most recent visit to Sydney we mentioned to him how much we wanted to see a saffron festival in Consuegra.

I am delighted to say we recently received the following email:

> Dear Ian and Liz,
> How are you and the family? I hope you are doing well. We are fine but getting warmer and warmer, summer time is very close.
> Saffron's Festival
> The festival will be the last week of October but the main dates are Saturday 26th and Sunday 27th. I think we should get there on Friday 25th during the day to take a look around to know how to move and where to go and Saturday morning to start at the festival.
> I will give you more information later but meantime you can start preparing your visit to Spain.
> Best regards to all of you,
> Your friend,
> Pepe Sanchez

We are arranging the tickets and we can't wait to pack our bags.

SUGGESTED READING

Cherikoff, V., *The Bushfood Handbook*, Ti Tree Press, Australia, 1997

Cribb, A.B. & J.W., *Wild Food in Australia*, William Collins, Sydney, 1975

Else, D., *Zanzibar: The Bradt Travel Guide*, Bradt Publications, UK. Bradt travel guides are updated regularly.

Gernot Katzner Spice Pages, www.ang.kfunigraz.ac.at/~katzner/index.html

Grieve, M., *A Modern Herbal Vol. 1 & 2*, Hafner Publishing Co., New York, 1959

Hemphill, I., *Spice Notes*, Pan Macmillan Australia, Sydney, 2002

Hemphill, J. & R., *Hemphills' Herbs: Their Cultivation and Usage*, Lansdowne Press, Sydney, 1983

Humphries, J., *The Essential Saffron Companion*, Ten Speed Press, California, 1998

Latz, P.K., *Bushfires and Bushtucker*, IAD Press, Alice Springs, 1996

Let's Go travel guides to Greece and Turkey, Macmillan, USA. Let's Go guides are updated annually.

Lonely Planet travel guides to India, Sri Lanka, Vietnam and Spain, Lonely Planet Publications, Melbourne. Lonely Planet guides are updated regularly.

Mitchell, K., A Spice Merchant with a Hanoi Twist, MSNBC 'Global Entrepreneurs', http://www.prettygoodwriter.com/msnbc/spice.html

Perikos, J., *The Chios Gum Mastic*, John Perikos, Chios, Greece, 1993

Pruthi, J.S., *Spices and Condiments: Chemistry, Microbiology, Technology*, Academic Press, London, 1980

Robins, J., *Wild Lime*, Allen & Unwin, St Leonards, 1998

Rushdie, S., *The Moor's Last Sigh*, Jonathan Cape, London, 1995

Smith, K. & I., *Grow Your Own Bushfoods*, New Holland Publishers, Sydney, 1999

Spices Board India (Ministry of Commerce Govt. of India), *Indian Spices: a Catalogue*, Cochin, 1992

Vogel, S., *Teotihuacan History, Art and Monuments*, Monclem Ediciones, S.A. de C.V., 1995

ACKNOWLEDGMENTS

Spice Travels has given me a wonderful opportunity to share many of the spice experiences I have had while in pursuit of my passion, an interest nurtured by my parents for nearly as long as I can remember. My fascination with this ancient and intoxicating trade could not have been satisfied without the generosity and hospitality of many growers, traders and food lovers, who share this interest.

Among the people who have been so helpful over the years, I would particularly like to thank Dr P.S.S. Thampi, Director of Publicity, Spices Board of India. I met Thampi in 1986 at the First International Spice Group Meeting in New Delhi, and since then he has made it possible for us to visit numerous spice-growing, research and processing facilities in India, and he has also become a dear and valued friend. My thanks also go to Thampi's friends, who befriended us and made us feel so welcome during our stay in Cochin. Dr Anthony Katticaran and his wife Jansi, who made sure Stegie fed us on delectable south Indian food every day. We will never forget the late Bobby Hormis and his wife Annie. Bobby was one of the warmest and most fun-loving people we have met, and he is sadly missed by all who knew him. We had a wonderful experience and learnt so much from Mr Sathyanarayana (Satir), at whose farmhouse we stayed when he showed us around the organic spice farms in Mangalore. Travelling to the south of India would not be the same without Johnson Teju, a professional tourist guide who specialises in Kerala, and accompanies our Spice Tours with charm and incredible local knowledge.

Others to whom I am indebted are the Gaya family in Papantla, Mexico, for introducing us to vanilla in its native habitat, and Craig Semple and his associate Yomi, who arranged for us to meet the sumac producers in Nizip. We were overwhelmed in Vietnam by the generosity of Mark Barnett, his wife Yen and their staff in Hanoi, and the delightful Dzoanh and his wife Oanh who showed us the cassia forests in Khe Dua.

My thanks also go to Janet and Roy Chisholm of Napperby Station in Central Australia, who not only excelled at country hospitality, but made it possible for me to meet with members of the local Aboriginal community. There I saw many varieties of Australian native foods and experienced the joy of gathering bush tomatoes, and witchetty grubs, with Kitty Cockatoo and her friends.

A book like this would never have been written without the support and persistence of my agent, Philippa Sandall and the enthusiasm of my publisher, Bernadette Foley of Pan

Macmillan Australia. To my editor Brianne Tunnicliffe, and also to Mark Evans, Jody Lee and Deborah Parry, thank you for your patience and attention to detail.

And of course I could not have written this book without the encouragement of my wife Liz. She has endured many so-called holidays in remote, uncomfortable, steamy, mosquito-ridden (but never inhospitable) parts of the world, while humouring my obsession with spices. She is my greatest supporter and most constructive critic; her natural commonsense and innate editorial skills have been invaluable.

Finally, Liz and I would not have been able to travel if it wasn't for the support we get from our wonderful staff, and our loyal customers. We can confidently venture into an inaccessible jungle knowing that Anna Blunt, Jacquie Newling and the team (including our daughter Sophie who takes time off from her studies to help) will keep things running smoothly.

Ian Hemphill
Spice Notes

The culmination of a life's work, *Spice Notes* is Ian Hemphill's definitive guide to culinary herbs and spices.

Beginning with the history of this ancient trade, Ian Hemphill takes the reader on a fascinating tour through the cultures and cuisines of the spice world.

Providing detailed information on all the herbs and spices used in today's cooking, and including over fifty blue-print recipes for inspiration, *Spice Notes* is a classic work for every kitchen.

Acclaim for *Spice Notes*

Published in 2000, *Spice Notes* was

The winner of the Best Hard-Cover Food-related Book, in the Vittoria Australian Food Writers Awards of 2001

Nominee in the Jacob's Creek Best Hard-Cover Food Book category in the Jacob's Creek 2001 World Food Media Awards

Listed in the top 100 'favourite foods, restaurants, recipes, people, places and things' in America's *Saveur* magazine